The Slot Machine Answer Book

The Slot Machine Answer Book

How They Work, How They've Changed and How to Overcome the House Advantage

Second Edition

John Grochowski

Bonus Books
Los Angeles, California

© 1999, 2005 by Bonus Books
All rights reserved

ISBN (second edition): 1-56625-235-0

The Library of Congress has cataloged the first edition as follows:

Grochowski, John
     The slot machine answer book : how they work, how they've changed, and how to overcome the house advantage / John Grochowski.
        p.   cm.
     Includes bibliographical references.
     ISBN 1-56625-120-8
     1. Slot machines—Handbooks, manuals, etc.   I. Title.
   TJ1570.G76   1999   99-17731
795.2'7—dc21   CIP

09   08   07   06   05   5   4   3   2   1

Bonus Books
1223 Wilshire Blvd. #597
Santa Monica, CA 90403

Printed in the United States of America

Contents

Acknowledgments

Keeping up with the latest in slot games and the way the machines work means a constant quest for new information. Much comes from the slot manufacturers themselves. I couldn't have done this book without guided tours of booths at gaming shows, along with interviews originally done for magazines and my newspaper column with IGT's Ed Rogich, Bally Gaming's Marcus Prater, WMS Gaming's Larry Pacey, Aristocrat's Kent Young, Atronic's Jason Stage and Katie Stage, and many more. Fellow authors Frank Scoblete and John Robison have long been a great deal of help. My editors, including Marian Green at *Slot Manager* and *International Gaming and Wagering Business,* John Busam and Catherine Jaeger at *Midwest Gaming and Travel,* and Miriam DiNunzio at the *Chicago Sun-Times* have sent me down many a path to learn more about the games we play. And, as always, biggest thanks go to my wife, Marcy, for all the help, patience and kind words that ease the task of meeting deadlines.

Introduction

Walking down the corridor of the Las Vegas Convention Center in the fall of 2003, I passed a couple of Jedi knights, lightsabers at their sides. I made a left turn to enter the display floor of the Global Gaming Expo, and there was Marilyn Monroe—or at least a reasonable facsimile.

A little farther along, one of the Blues Brothers handed me a pair of sunglasses. Apparently I was too early for actors Kevin Nealon and Dan Aykroyd, but no matter. A day earlier the cast had included *Gilligan's Island* castaways Bob Denver, Dawn Wells and Russell Johnson, *I Dream of Jeannie*'s magical Barbara Eden, comedians Rip Torn and Jeff Foxworthy, and Laverne and Shirley themselves, Penny Marshall and Cindy Williams. On their way were eternal teenager Dick Clark, *M*A*S*H* company clerk Gary Berghoff, *Dilbert* cartoonist Scott Adams and one more castaway, Tina Louise, and the following day would bring *Dating Game* host Jim Lange.

What could bring together such a gathering of pop culture icons? Slot machines.

Slots for the new millennium aren't just about landing three 7s on the reels. They're about fun. Casinos are selling us entertainment just as much as they're holding out the hope of a jackpot. And the bonus rounds, extra spins, games within a game, characters and animation on modern slot machines are a lot more fun than just watching the reels.

When I was writing the first edition of *The Slot Machine Answer Book* way back in 1998 and '99, the slot machine industry was just about a century old—and, at the same time, it was in its infancy.

From the time of the first three-reel machine—and in the fourth set of answers in this book's 10 "Reel Spin" quizzes, we'll see just what that groundbreaking game was—slot play had stayed more or less the same. Drop your coins in the slot, pull the handle or push the button, and watch the reels spin to see if you win.

It's a far different world today. Slots today have bonus rounds and second events. There are extras built into the top boxes while the reels spin below. On an ever-increasing share of games, the reels are on video screens, and those screens sometimes replace the reels with animated scenes of vegetable-growing contests or fishing derbies or dancing chickens, all while awarding players bonus payoffs.

Pop culture themes have taken over the casinos. As I walk through a modern slot floor, I can stop to answer trivia questions on *Ripley's Believe It or Not,* spin the bonus wheel on *Wheel of Fortune,* take a turn around the board in Monopoly or drop the Plinko disk on *The Price Is Right.*

If I choose, I can also spin the reels and wait to see if I can line up three 7s or three bars.

The explosion of player choice started to reach the public in the mid-1990s, a few years after the legalization of Indian gaming and riverboat casinos took casino gambling outside its Nevada and New Jersey homes. Slot machines, once a mere sidelight while the serious gambling was done at the tables, had become the casinos' most played and most profitable games. Casinos and their suppliers needed to provide an entertaining experience to keep slot players coming back.

What happened was a revolution. Anchor Gaming devised a bonus wheel that fit atop regular slot machines, and when the winning symbol appeared on the reels the player could press a button to spin the wheel and win the bonus amount indicated when it stopped. Anchor's Wheel of Gold launched a bevy of bonus-wheel games, and IGT's *Wheel of Fortune,* based on the TV game show, became one of the most successful slot machine lines in history.

Start-up company Silicon Gaming went the high-tech route with its Odyssey games, putting the spinning reels on an oversize video screen, and building in bonus events that would transform the reels into the vault at Fort Knox or a gypsy's den.

WMS Gaming went video, too, after some stops and starts with its reel-spinning slots. It started by building bonus rounds into reel slots by putting a Dotmation screen on the top box—in the early hit Piggy Bankin', landing the piggy bank on the reels would break the bank on the screen, releasing bonus coins. But, when WMS found itself in a patent dispute and a judge ruled the company could not distribute reel-spinning games, it followed the lead of Australian manufacturers and designed video slots with five "reels," bonus rounds and a high frequency of winning spins. When players flocked to WMS's Reel 'Em In, the slot machine industry was changed forever. Since the mid-1990s, video slots have been the fastest-growing segment of the casino world, and they'll stand on their own as the subject of my upcoming *Video Slot Machine Answer Book.*

Today's bonuses and games-within-games, in both reel-spinning and video formats, take me back to a conversation with the slot director of one of the new riverboat casinos in the early 1990s. The casino industry was changing, not only in breaking out of its long-time Nevada and New Jersey homes to bring gaming to riverboats and Native American reservations across the nation, but also in the way it was presented to the public. Suddenly, casinos were an entertainment option for all adults, and they were reaching out to people who had never played before. Bids to bring customers in the door grew beyond the brashness of neon. Now the fairy-tale castle exterior of Excalibur and the pyrotechnics of the volcano at the Mirage sent a message to visitors: "Come in. Try your hand. It's fun here."

Slot machines were another matter. They weren't evolving as fast as the industry itself, and at least one slot director worried about disappointing the customers once they came in the door.

"The one thing that disappoints me is the slot product itself," she told me. "Everything we're doing in this industry is aimed at making it more fun for the players, but we're still putting the same kind of slot product on the floor we were 10 years ago.

"Somebody needs to give the manufacturers a creative kick."

Somewhere, somehow, the boot was applied, and now players are getting bigger kicks than ever out of the games. It's the player, after all, who is the real winner in this revolution. The payoff is in more entertainment value, more bang for the buck, more fun at the casino.

A chance to win a lifestyle-changing jackpot is still a prime allure of the slots, of course. But, more than ever before, we have players who are after a day's entertainment, a little fun and maybe, just maybe, a chance to walk away a winner.

In this book, we'll look at slot machines and what makes them tick. We'll check out some trivia and history, myths and percentages, and even ways to occasionally get ahead of the game.

About the Answer Books

This is a browser's book, arranged in 10 "Reel Spins" with questions about slot machines. There are multiple choice questions, definitions, true and false, even a couple of matching games. Much more than a book of questions, this is a book of answers. Look up the answer to a multiple-choice question, and you'll find more than just A, B or C. The questions are jump-off points for mini-essays, excuses to go off on tangents and relate casino experiences and things I've learned while looking up other things.

Do you have to take the quizzes to enjoy the book? No. You can just as easily read the answers as a series of essays about slot machines. Many readers of my Answer Book series have told me they enjoy being challenged by the questions. Others say the answers are really what they're after.

By the time you've read to the finish—or jumped around until you've read just about everything—you'll have learned quite a lot about slot machines past and present. And, more than that, I hope you'll have had fun, because that's what slot machines in this age are all about.

Reel Spin No. 1: Definitions

Is a slot machine an electronic gaming device, or is an electronic gaming device a slot machine? Can you distinguish between a symbol and a stop?

Here are a few terms we'll be using over and over again. See if you know just what we mean by the following:

1. **Slot machine**
2. **Electronic gaming device**
3. **Loose slot**
4. **Tight slot**
5. **Payline**
6. **Pay table**
7. **Window**
8. **Credit meter**
9. **Symbol**
10. **Stop**
11. **Handle pull**
12. **Payback percentage**
13. **Hold percentage**
14. **Hopper**
15. **Hopper fill**

16. **Random number generator**

17. **Mechanical slot machine**

18. **Progressive meter**

19. **Second screen**

20. **Scatter pay**

Reel Spin No. 1: Definitions Answers

1. Slot machines are casino gaming devices that spin reels— whether the reels are moving parts or images on a video screen—to determine the outcome of a wager.

Simple enough, right? No trick questions this early.

But, just to clear up any misconceptions about the games we're talking about, let's go through a little of what slot machines do and do not include:

Slot machines do not all have coin slots.

Slot machines began as coin-operated devices, and most still have a coin head with a slot through which players insert coins to activate play. But nearly all modern slot machines also have a bill validator that allows players to insert currency rather than coins. And the wave of the future is to do away with coins and tokens altogether. That future is already here in many casinos, which have machines with ticket printers. Push the button to cash out, and you get a bar-coded ticket that you can either insert in a bill validator to get credits on another machine, or take to the cashiers' cage to exchange for cash.

Some casino executives are already looking to the day the printers themselves will be obsolete. The ultimate goal—at least until the next ultimate goal comes along—is to use "smart cards," with magnetic strips like credit cards, to transfer funds. Use the card to put credits on the slot, then transfer credits back to the card when you cash out.

Still, the games that use such coinless technology have spinning reels, or video screens with images of spinning reels. That's the essence of slot machine games, even if they don't have slots.

One-armed bandits they may be, but slot machines don't necessarily have arms.

Traditionally, slot machines have had arms on the right side, and players would pull the arms to start play. The arm is window dressing on today's slots—pulling the handle doesn't physically push the gears to move the reels anymore. A pull on the handle just triggers the same electronic relay you'd activate if you pushed the button marked "Spin Reels" or "Max Coins" instead. Most modern slots forgo the handle altogether—all play is activated by pushing buttons.

In recent years, "slant-top" slots have grown in popularity. Slant tops sit lower to the ground than upright models, have a wider base and often are more comfortable places to sit. These machines are installed flush against each other, with no room for a handle. Playing the slant tops is entirely a matter of pushing buttons and not pulling handles, but they're still slot machines.

By "slot machines," we don't mean video poker, video blackjack, video keno or any other coin- or currency-activated gaming devices.

Casino statistics do lump together all these games and more. In answers about the number of slot machines in use or average payback percentages, we'll have to consider all these different games as slot machines, and that will be noted.

However, most of the answers in this book, including those about how the machines work and methods of play, will be specifically about the machines defined here as slots. Those who are interested in video poker and video blackjack might enjoy my *The Casino Answer Book* and *The Video Poker Answer Book*. Video keno, as well as live keno, is a subject for another time.

2. Electronic gaming devices are all coin- or currency-activated electronic games on which players may place wagers. That's the catch-all term that includes video poker, video blackjack and video keno as well as slot machines. It also includes electronic horse racing games such as Sigma Derby, the Flip-It games in which players try to send coins cascading over the edges of metal shelves, craps machines, video roulette or any other oddball electronic games you might find in a casino.

The games can be fun. My wife Marcy has a weakness for Flip-It, but has never gotten much return and usually restrains herself to a sigh and a moment of "Oh, I know I shouldn't, but I *like* those games," before taking a pass. One night when nothing was going right for me on any other casino game, I whiled away an inexpensive hour on Sigma Derby and kept myself entertained.

But these games are not what we mean by slot machines.

3. A **loose slot** is a machine that's loose with its money—it gives back a lot to the players. They're also called liberal slots or hot slots, in casino hyperbole. A loose slot doesn't always seem loose. Even the best-paying machines have periods during which they seem to be pinching every nickel, quarter or dollar.

I once took a casino operations class during which a slot department executive gave us a behind-the-scenes tour, and mentioned a particular bank of $1 slots, "These are our loosest machines. Very hot."

One of the women in our group played them that night, and reported, "He was right about those machines. I won $400, then a little while later I hit for another $600." She was thrilled.

I decided to give it a try, and that second night I slipped $100 into the bill validator. Playing the machine's maximum of two coins per pull, I sent the reels spinning 50 times. Twice I hit three "any bars" for a net return of $20. Forty-eight times, my return was zero.

For me, that particular slot was far from loose. That's a normal part of the game. Loose slots have long losing streaks, too, and to win not only do you have to be in the right place, you have to be there at the right time.

4. Tight slots are the opposite of loose slots—they hold onto your money and keep it for the casino.

Usually, you'll find the slots looser in areas with a lot of competition and tighter in areas with just one or two isolated casinos. Casinos in downtown Las Vegas, which not only compete with each other but also try to lure customers away from the glamour of the Strip, tend to have loose slots, with quarter machines that pay about 2 percent more in the long run than electronic gaming devices on the Strip. Slots are tighter in New Jersey, where casino locations don't lead to the same door-to-door casino hopping you'll find in Nevada. Atlantic City casinos average less than a 91 percent return on quarter slots, about 2 percent less than the return on the Las Vegas Strip.

5. For us to win on most slot machines, symbols must land on a **payline,** a line painted across the glass on machines with physical reels or present as a video image on video slots. If a machine will pay us 1,000 coins for three 7s, the 7s must land so the payline appears to be running through them. If any of the 7s are just above or just below the payline, it's a losing spin.

Some machines have more than one payline. Three-payline machines, with three horizontal lines across the glass, are very common. Usually, a three-payline machine will take up to three coins at a time, and each coin activates a payline. If you play two coins, and your three 7s land on the third payline, you do not win.

Video slots with five reel images can have 5, 9, 10, 15, 20 or more paylines. To use the simplest example, on a five-line game the paylines include the three horizontal lines across the glass, a "V" connecting the top of left-hand reel, the bottom of the third reel and the top of the fifth reel, and an upside-down "V" connecting the bottom of the first reel, the top of the third and the bottom of the fifth. With more paylines, the lines zig and zag—for example, connecting the symbols on the tops of the first and second reels, middle of the third reel and bottoms of the fourth and fifth. The lines are usually color coded, and touching the "Help" button on the screen will usually show you how the paylines are drawn.

No matter how many paylines, you must bet at least one coin per line to activate them all. If you bet only four coins on a five-payline machine, you lose if a winning combination hits on the fifth payline. It is also possible to bet more than one coin per line on these machines. Games from the Australian manufacturer Aristocrat sometimes have 20 paylines that will accept bets up to 10 coins per line—a 200-coin maximum bet.

6. The **pay table** tells you how many coins winning spins pay. On machines with physical reels, the pay table is painted on the machine glass, usually on the top panel above the reels, although some games have the pay table on the bottom panel, below the slot.

On video games, the player usually has to press a button to see the pay table on the screen. Most units have buttons to press to see a "Help" menu for game explanations, and some have a separate "pay table" button. There usually are physical buttons to push on the metal strip adjacent to the coin slot, but there are also images of "Help" and "pay table" buttons on the screen. Video slots use touch-screen technology, and the player can see the pay table just by touching "pay table" on the screen. An image of a "return to game" button then appears on the screen to allow you to go back at will.

7. The **window** is the glass through which we can see the reels on a slot machine. Usually we can see not only the symbols that land on the payline, but also one above the payline and one below. And, if we really strain, on some machines we can stare along the curve of the reel and see a second symbol above and a second symbol below the payline.

Ignore them. If the symbol is not on the payline, it doesn't do you any good, and it has no impact on subsequent spins.

8. Not very long ago, all slot machines dropped all your winnings immediately into a tray at the bottom of the machine. If you hit three bars and won 30 coins, 30 coins would come clanking into the tray.

Today's machines allow you to build credits instead. If you hit three bars and win 30 coins, 30 coins will be added to the **credit meter,** an electronic display that tells you how many coins you have remaining.

Start by sliding currency into a bill validator, and that amount of money is added to the credit meter. Sit down at a traditional quarter three-reel machine with zero credits, slide a $20 bill into the bill validator and 80 credits, representing 80 quarters, appear on the credit meter.

Instead of dropping coins into the slot, the player with credits on the meter then pushes a "Max Bet" button, or a "Bet One Coin" button followed by a "Spin Reels" button. If the player has 80 credits on a machine that takes up to three coins at a time and hits "Max Bet," the credit meter will go down to 77, the reels will spin, and if the spin is a winner additional credits will be added to the meter.

9. See 10.

10. Let's look at **"symbols"** and **"stops"** together. "Symbols" are the cherries, bars, double bars, triple bars, 7s or any other images the slot manufacturer uses on its reels. They'll often fit in with the theme of the game—*The Munsters* uses images of Herman, Lily, Grandpa, Eddie and Marilyn, and Fortune Cookie uses carryout boxes, "Good Luck" signs and, yes, fortune cookies. If the right combination of symbols lands on the payline, the player has a winner.

But symbols don't always land on the payline. Sometimes the payline runs through spaces between symbols. Any point on the reel that can land on a payline is a "stop."

11. In casino terminology, every play, every spin of the reels, is a **handle pull.** It doesn't matter if you push a button instead of pulling the handle. It doesn't even matter if you're sitting in the Space-Quest casino at the Las Vegas Hilton and pass your hand through a beam to start the spin instead. Every play is a handle pull.

A casino marketer who had worked for both the Harrah's and Trump organizations once told me that, in Atlantic City, they figured customers played at about 240 handle pulls per hour. Now that players aren't dropping coins into the slot for every play and are pushing buttons instead of pulling the handle, play is much faster—I usually figure 400 to 500 pulls per hour as a steady pace, with as many as 1,000 pulls per hour possible for someone who keeps hitting "Max Bet" as rapidly as he can.

12. The **payback percentage** is the percentage of all money played that is returned to players. It varies widely from machine to machine, casino to casino and state to state. If we talk about payback percentages on dollar slots, we have to specify where we mean—they return better than 95 percent in Nevada or Mississippi, but closer to 94 percent in Indiana and 93 percent in New Jersey.

Payback percentages are figured over the long haul, hundreds of thousands of handle pulls. You may be sitting at a machine that returns 95 percent, but that doesn't mean that after playing $100 you'll have $95 left. In such a short trial, you could have $50, or $20, or even zero. You could also have $100, $200 or even have hit a big jackpot worth thousands. In the long run, through thousands of players, it balances out.

Most players get a bigger percentage back from the machine than they think they're getting. They forget that they're getting some payback as they go, and that they're getting much more play than their original buy-in.

Let's say you slide $100 into the bill validator. The first time you play it through, you get three mixed bars for $10 per hit three times and three single bars for $20 twice. You have only $70 left, and when you run that through you get three mixed bars three times and single bars once for a total return of $50. Play that and you get three double bars for $40, but no other hits. Then you get single bars once and any bars once for $30, any bars twice for $20, single bars once for $20, any bars once for $10. And then you lose your last $10. Just like that, you've lost $100. It's probably only taken 15 minutes.

"I didn't hit *anything*," you complain. "It just sucked down my money."

To you, it feels like a zero percent payback.

How big was the real payback percentage? Well, the machine was cold, but not quite as frigid as you thought. You played $100 the first time through, then $70, $50, $40, $30, $20, $20 and $10.

Your total play is $340. You've gotten returns of $70, $50, $40, $30, $20, $20 and $10 for a total of $240. Divide the $240 in returns by $340 and you find the payback percentage on this iceberg was 70.6 percent.

That's zero in your wallet, but 70.6 percent when the casino reports the statistics.

13. The **hold percentage** is just the flip side of the payback percentage. It's how casino operators look at the data when analyzing their own bottom lines. They may tell you, "Our slots average 95 percent payback," but behind closed doors they tell each other, "Our slots are holding 5 percent." It's the same number looked at from the opposite side.

14. The **hopper** is the device that circulates coins out of a pool to allow the machine to pay you off—on machines that still pay off in coins or tokens. When you push the "cash out" button, the hopper circulates coins to be dropped into the tray.

15. A **hopper fill** is what's needed when there aren't enough coins in the hopper to pay you off. A light flashes on top of the machine and an attendant is signaled to open the cabinet and pour coins into the hopper. On video games, a message will flash on the screen saying, "Hopper Empty. Call Attendant."

There was an attempt in the '90s to make hopper fills something of an entertainment experience. Silicon Gaming designed its high-tech Odyssey games to play a live-action video explaining that an attendant has been alerted and someone will be right there. "In the meantime," the actor in the video announces, "I think we should watch this." A video plays listings of casino promotions, or a series of trivia questions appear on the screen, all helping the player pass time until the attendant arrives.

That's probably the only attempt we'll see at making hopper fills fun, with the trend toward replacing hoppers with ticket printers.

16. The **random number generator,** or RNG, is the computer program that determines what is going to show up on the symbols. It continuously generates numbers corresponding to reel combinations, even when the machine is not in use. All it does is generate the numbers; it is not on the same chip as the game graphics, the coin counters or the slot club tracking system. It does not know how many coins you've played, how long it's been since you last won or whether you're playing with a slot club card. It just generates numbers, and if you're lucky enough it's generating a winning number at the same microsecond that you're signaling the machine that you're about to play by pulling the handle, or by hitting the "Spin Reels" or "Max Bet" button.

The RNG is the key to unraveling much of the mythology and confusion that surrounds the way slot machines work. We'll be referring to it again in subsequent chapters.

17. The slot-machine-as-computer that rules the casino world today is a relatively recent innovation. Through the 1950s, mechanical slot machines ruled the roost. **Mechanical slots** were almost clockwork devices. The handle, which today is just a decoration harking back to the old days, then actually was the device that started the reels spinning.

On mechanical machines, the number of symbols and spaces on the reels determine jackpot odds. If there were 10 symbols and 10 spaces on each reel, yielding 20 stops, and there was one 7 on each real, the odds of hitting three 7s were 1 in 20 x 20 x 20, or 1 in 8,000. That limited the size of the jackpot. Today's multimillion-dollar slot jackpots could never have been offered on a mechanical machine—to hold enough symbols to make the odds high enough, the reels would have been too large to fit in the machine casing.

18. The **progressive meter** shows the size of the jackpot on machines that put a percentage of coins played in an ever-building jackpot. There are some one-machine progressives, in which a lighted meter on the machine itself shows the jackpot building as you play. More common today are linked progressives, in which several machines are linked by computer so that a percentage of coins played in all machines at the bank are added to a common jackpot. Sometimes, machines in different casinos are linked together, as in the IGT Megabucks games with multimillion-dollar jackpots. When the link involves several casinos, the games are called wide-area progressives. Usually, a lighted sign atop the bank of machines tracks the size of the jackpot for all.

19. Video slots almost always have **second screens,** meaning that, when the player hits a bonus combination on the video reels, the image of reels fades off the screen and is replaced by another image—a second screen. In WMS's breakthrough game Reel 'Em In, for example, when the player hits three fishing lures of the same type on consecutive reels, a scene of five fishing boats on a pond appears. The player chooses one fisherman to reel in his bonus jackpot.

That was an early, simple bonus round. Today, games often have multiple bonus rounds, and bonus rounds with multiple levels. Sometimes they use animation and even film clips, as in IGT's *Star Wars,* where players fight space battles, targeting opposing warriors and ships.

20. Machines that offer a **scatter pay** give the players a payoff when certain symbols appear anywhere in the slot window, even if they don't line up on the same payline.

Slot machines that offer scatter pays, second screens, multiple paylines and take multiple coins per line are often referred to as "Australian-style slots." Australian slot players have gone big for advanced video machines, to the extent that they are much more common Down Under than traditional reel-spinners. U.S. casinos have been increasing the share devoted to video, but there remains a much stronger base devoted to reel-spinning games here. In researching a magazine article in 2001, I had a casino slot director tell me that his ideal slot floor would have half video and half reel-spinning product. And, in 2003, a slot manager at a Native American casino told me he had in excess of 40 percent video slots on his floor. Video slots eventually will take over more than half the space devoted to slot machines in the United States, but reel slots seem destined to be with us a good long time.

Reel Spin No. 2: What and Where

What ranks as king of the casino—blackjack, craps, roulette or slot machines? Just how many slots are in use, anyway? And where are our favorite places to play?

Try your hand at these multiple-choice tidbits before you check out the answers.

1. **In the United States, slot machines rank as:**
   A. The most popular casino game.
   B. The second most popular casino game, behind blackjack.
   C. The third most popular casino game, behind blackjack and craps.
   D. The fourth most popular casino game, behind blackjack, craps and roulette.

2. **In the United States, slot machines account for:**
   A. About 40 percent of casino revenue.
   B. About 50 percent of casino revenue.
   C. About 60 percent of casino revenue.
   D. More than 70 percent of casino revenue.

3. **The number of slot machines in use in the United States is:**
   A. More than 200,000.
   B. More than 300,000.
   C. More than 400,000.
   D. More than 500,000.

4. **The most common coins or tokens played in U.S. slot machines are worth:**
   A. 5 cents.
   B. 25 cents.
   C. 50 cents.
   D. One dollar.

5. **Dollar slots:**
   A. Earn about half as much for the casino as quarter slots.
   B. Earn about the same amount for the casino as quarter slots
   C. Earn about twice as much for the casino as quarter slots.
   D. Earn about four times as much for the casino as quarter slots.

6. **Nickel slots, once the most-played machines in the U.S., now:**
   A. Are nearly extinct.
   B. Are restricted to a few small casinos.
   C. Are making a comeback.
   D. Remain as popular as ever.

7. **Penny slots:**
   A. Died out in the 1980s.
   B. Now exist only in "The Copper Mine" at the Gold Spike in Las Vegas.
   C. Are widespread at limited gaming sites in North Dakota.
   D. Are coming back.

8. **There are more slot machines on the Las Vegas Strip:**
   A. Than in the rest of the United States combined.
   B. Than in the rest of Nevada combined.
   C. Than in any two gaming states outside Nevada combined.
   D. Than in any gaming state outside Nevada.

9. **Outside Nevada, the state with the most slot machines is:**
   A. New Jersey.
   B. Mississippi.

   C. Illinois.

   D. Missouri.

10. The casino with the most slot machines is in:

   A. Nevada.

   B. New Jersey.

   C. Connecticut.

   D. Indiana.

11. The Midwestern state in which slot machines remained illegal for a time after casinos were legalized is:

   A. Illinois.

   B. Missouri.

   C. Indiana.

   D. Iowa.

12. Slot machines in Midwestern riverboat states differ from those in Nevada, New Jersey and Mississippi in that:

   A. Payback percentages are lower.

   B. Payback percentages are higher.

   C. Slots accept casino tokens, not U.S. coins, at all denominations.

   D. Progressive games that link jackpots at competing casinos are illegal.

13. In recent years, the number of slot machine manufacturers has:

   A. Increased.

   B. Decreased through merger and consolidation.

   C. Stayed about the same.

14. In order to place their slot machines in casinos, manufacturers must:

   A. Submit competitive bids under state vendor guidelines.

   B. Be licensed by state gaming boards.

   C. Have individual machines approved by state legislatures.

   D. All of the above.

15. A "field test":

A. Places a new machine in a casino or a few casinos on a limited basis.

B. Is a demonstration in which the manufacturer takes a machine in an electronically-equipped van for inspection by casino operators.

C. Places new slots in a casino office, where selected customers are invited to play for free and give opinions on the game.

16. The majority of slot players play games that:

A. Have progressive jackpots.

B. Have three physical reels and accept two or three coins per play.

C. Have reels on a video screen and accept two or three coins per play.

D. Have reels on a video screen and accept 45 or more coins per play.

17. The largest slot jackpot ever hit in the United States is:

A. $9 million.

B. $19 million.

C. $29 million.

D. $39 million.

18. Among casino games in the 1950s, slot machines ranked:

A. First in popularity.

B. Second in popularity.

C. Third in popularity.

D. Fourth in popularity.

19. In European casinos, slot machines are:

A. Even more popular than in the U.S.

B. Less popular than in the U.S.

C. About as popular as in the U.S.

20. When slot reels are on video screens:

A. Players avoid them like the plague.

B. The games have a tougher time finding a market.

C. The games once had a tough time finding a market, but are rapidly increasing in popularity.

Reel Spin No. 2: What and Where Answers

1. A. Slot machines rank as the most popular casino game in the United States, with blackjack and video poker running neck-and-neck for second.

When states release slot statistics they lump together all types of machines as "electronic gaming devices." So in subsequent answers when we discuss the numbers of slots in use or revenue from slots, keep in mind that statistics include video poker, video blackjack, video keno, Flip-It and other games as well as those we usually consider slots. As a rule of thumb, figure reel slots, whether they have physical reels or reels on a video screen, account for about 80 percent of electronic gaming devices, with most of the remainder being video poker.

There are lots of reasons for the popularity of slot machines. The eye-catching lights and graphics and ear-catching sound systems on the newest machines draw the players right in to see what all the excitement's about. The atmosphere around the slots is electric. This is where someone might hit a jackpot worth thousands, even millions of dollars for an investment of only a few coins. But any win is exciting. You'll hear players screaming with delight, and neighbors cheering them on, for a win of a couple hundred nickels that wouldn't even turn a head at the tables.

But the most important reason probably is just that the slots are easy to play. Just drop a coin or slide a few bucks into a bill validator, push a button to spin the reels, and wait for your result. Time and again, I've had casino newcomers complain to me about a harried dealer who wouldn't explain how to play, or surly players who jump all over a novice who makes a bad play.

A friend of mine, a bright, confident, assertive—and some of her subjects might even say aggressive and pushy—newspaper reporter, once decided to try her hand at the blackjack table.

"I couldn't believe those people," she told me afterward. "How can you stand it? Every time I made a play this one guy didn't like, he snarled at me. I took a card he didn't think I should have, the dealer made a 21 and he started yelling about players who don't know what they're doing. Half the table looked at me like I was from outer space.

"That was enough. Back to the slots for me."

The slots are a safe haven, a place to play for someone who doesn't want to worry about mistakes that might affect the wagers of others. A slot player only has to worry about his own bankroll.

2. D. Slot machines account for more than 70 percent of casino revenue. In some jurisdictions, more than 80 percent of casino revenue comes from the slots, and in other places it's pushing 90 percent. In Las Vegas, where tables still accounted for more than half of casino revenue at the dawn of the 1980s, slots machines' share pushed past 65 percent in the early years of the new millennium. In Illinois in 2002, slots accounted for more than 84 percent of $1.8 billion in casino revenue.

That's a far cry from the way things were just 30 years ago. In the late 1960s, table games accounted for 80 percent or more of casino revenue. Serious gambling was done at the tables. Slots were an amusement for those accompanying table players to the casino. Casinos didn't count on slot machines for big profits, not with most machines taking nickels one coin at a time, with fewer taking quarters and silver dollars. The tables were the profit center.

"The big players sometimes came alone, and sometimes brought their wives or girlfriends," an acquaintance who was a pit boss in that era told me. "The hosts would give the wives and girlfriends rolls of nickels so they could entertain themselves at the slots. We didn't see many women at the tables. Nowadays it's different. The women are shooting craps with the men, and the men are playing slots with the women."

Change could hardly be more dramatic than what's happened in the last few decades. Now slot machines are the profit center, and the number of tables is dwindling. Slots still take nickels, quarters and dollar tokens, but they also take $5, $25, $100, even $1,000 tokens. I don't remember the last time I saw a machine that could accept only one coin per play; most take two, three and five, and now there are machines that take 45, 90, even 200 or more coins at a time.

No one in the casino industry today would ever suggest a slot player isn't a serious gambler. Slot players are among the casino's most important customers.

3. D. More than 500,000 slot machines are in use in the United States, and that number is growing all the time. As new gaming markets have opened, slot business has mushroomed. The opening of Native American casinos in California at the end of the 1990s and the beginning of the new millennium pushed the number past half a million, and Australian slotmaker Aristocrat estimated in 2000 that there would be 718,000 slots in use in the United States by 2010.

4. B. Quarter machines are by far the most common denomination in the United States, with more than 200,000 quarter machines in use. With the advent of video slots, nickels have replaced dollars as the second most common denomination, with more than 110,000 nickel games and close to 100,000 dollar machines in place.

In some newer gaming jurisdictions, especially on riverboat casinos, there are nearly as many dollar machines as there are quarter games. That's because of the space limitations that go with putting casinos on boats, and because of state restrictions on the number of gaming positions.

Illinois may be the best example. By law, the casinos on riverboats must move on the water, and each license is restricted to

1,200 gaming positions. Space is in short supply, and customer demand supports a greater percentage of dollar machines. Grand Victoria Casino in Elgin, Illinois, has more than 420 dollar slots, but fewer than 370 quarter machines. Hollywood Casino in Aurora and both Empress and Harrah's in Joliet all have more dollar machines than quarter machines.

That's a big contrast to the Nevada standard. Nevada, with plenty of space and intense competition prodding casinos to appeal to players at all levels, has about 60,000 quarter slots, and about 25,000 dollar machines. Meanwhile, nickel games, nearly extinct by the mid-1990s, have found new life thanks to video, with more than 35,000 games in Nevada casinos.

5. B. Even with fewer machines, dollar slots earn about as much for the casinos as quarter games and perhaps even a bit more.

There are a couple of factors at work. Dollar machines usually return more to the customer than quarter machines do. On the Las Vegas Strip, for example, about 93 percent of all money played in quarter machines is returned to the customer as winnings, while about 95 percent of the money wagered in dollar games goes back to the customer.

But 5 percent of a dollar is more money than 7 percent of a quarter, so on the average the casino keeps 5 cents for every coin bet in a dollar machine, and 1.75 cents for every coin bet in a quarter machine. That higher casino profit per pull balances out the larger number of quarter machines.

6. C. Nickel machines are making a comeback, fueled by the development of multiple-payline, multiple-coin video slots. In fact, nickel games rival quarters and dollars as the revenue leaders in modern casinos. Nickel machines, largely used for entertaining video games with lots of animation and bonus rounds, tend to keep players in their seats longer than reel-spinning games. They return a lower percentage of wagers to players. And average bet size is higher than you might think for games where 5 cents will buy you a spin of the video reels.

If a five-line machine accepts up to nine coins per line, then the player can wager as many as 45 coins per pull. Bet 45 nickels at a time, and you're wagering $2.25 per pull, up there in the rarified air with dollar slot players. If a 20-line machine accepts 10 coins per line, a maximum bet is 200 nickels, or $10 a spin. Now we're talking about the equivalent of two-coin $5 slots, true high rollers where extended play brings offers of complimentary room, food and beverage and plenty of other perks.

There's a risk for the casino that a player will play only one line and one coin at a time, taking up space and risking only 5 cents per pull. But while that certainly happens from time to time, casinos are finding most of their players on the new-wave nickel machines are betting much larger. The average seems to be about $1 to $1.25 per pull—more than the maximum wager on a three-coin quarter slot.

Let's take Indiana as an example, because the only nickel games there are multiline video slots, so we can see at a glance how these nickel bonus games compare with traditional quarter and dollar machines. In 2002, Indiana's 6,100 quarter machines at its 10 casinos produced $480 million in revenue, or nearly $79,000 per machine. There were fewer dollar games at 4,826 machines, but they actually produced more revenue, with $554 million, or nearly $115,000 per machine. There were fewer nickel games yet, with 4,118. They produced $437 million in revenue, or about $106 million per machine—far more per game than revenue on quarters, and nearly up to dollar standards.

7. D. Penny slots are coming back in a big way. Like the comeback by nickel machines, the return of penny games is driven by technology.

The key is cashless gaming. By 1998, Arizona Charlie's in Las Vegas had some penny slotless slot machines manufactured by

VLC—which in intervening years was absorbed by Anchor, which itself then was merged into slot giant IGT. They were among the earliest games to use ticket printers for cashouts, with no coins used at all. As in newer machines with ticket printers, the player bought in by inserting paper money in a bill validator, then cashed out by pushing a button to print out a ticket than could be redeemed with the cashier. Such systems save the casino time spent running coins through a counter, eliminate down time on machines for hopper fills and jams, and save the expense of buying a counter adapted to pennies.

Combine that with technology that allows the player to wager up to dozens and even hundreds of coins at a time, and suddenly the penny player isn't looked on as some vagabond one step from Skid Row.

"These aren't just penny slots," VLC's Mick Roemer explained to me at the time. "Denominations can be one cent, two cents, five cents, 10 cents, quarters. It's a coin-free environment that targets frequent gamblers, locals. It allows multidenomination, multiline play with no hopper."

Machines with no slot, machines that take 100 coins or more at a time and machines that allow a player to change from pennies to nickels to quarters to dollars without changing his seat are all part of what makes today's slot world exciting.

8. D. There are nearly 60,000 slot machines on the Las Vegas Strip, and the number is growing all the time. The opening of Bellagio late in 1998 and 1999 openings for Mandalay Bay and the Venitian kicked things up a notch, and the number of games continues to grow as casinos devote less space to tables and more to the more popular, profitable slots. The rest of Nevada has nearly 100,000 slots, but no other state with commercial gaming has more than about 40,000.

9. A. Outside Nevada, New Jersey has the most slot machines, although Mississippi is very close. New Jersey has roughly 40,000 slots, and Mississippi about 39,000. Other gaming states are relatively small by comparison—there are about 19,000 slots in Louisiana, 17,000 in Indiana, 15,000 each in Missouri and Colorado, nearly 13,000 in Connecticut, 12,000 in Iowa and 9,000 in Illinois. It's harder to get a handle on Native American gaming, where statistics aren't routinely made public, but California casinos were heading past 30,000 slots by 2003, probably the most among tribal gaming states.

10. C. The giant Foxwoods casino in Connecticut has the most slots in the United States, with nearly 6,600 as of mid-2003. The second most? Mohegan Sun, also in Connecticut, with 6,125.

11. B. Slot machines were illegal when casinos first opened in Missouri in 1994. Casino opponents found a provision in the state constitution barring games of chance that had been ignored during the approval and licensing process. Casinos were allowed to open with games of skill—blackjack, video poker and craps were designated as such. A later amendment allowed slots and other games of chance into the casinos.

12. C. Most Midwestern riverboat casinos use casino tokens and not U.S. coins in all electronic gaming devices. If you play a quarter slot machine in Nevada, New Jersey or Mississippi you can drop quarters into the slot, but play in Illinois, Iowa, Indiana or Missouri and you'll use non-negotiable casino tokens instead.

I once asked an Illinois regulator why tokens were used instead of coins, and I got a rambling response about a cashless environment protecting the integrity of gaming. No explanation of how the integrity of gaming is safeguarded by my dropping a 25-cent token into the slot instead of a good old American quarter, but there you go.

There actually is an element of protecting the integrity of gaming in the real reasons for tokens being used, but it's the integrity of accounting procedures the regulators are worried about.

Use of tokens in amounts less than a dollar started in Iowa with the launch of riverboat gaming in 1991. Iowa's original gaming law carried a $200 loss limit for players. To enforce the limit, Iowa developed a voucher system. With your boarding pass, you received $200 in vouchers, and to buy gaming chips or slot tokens, you had to present a voucher along with your money. If slot machines used U.S. coins, players could circumvent the law by bringing their own coins on board. So Iowa used tokens instead. That law has since been repealed, but Iowa and other riverboat states still use tokens instead of coins at all denominations.

From the casino's perspective, there are several good reasons to use tokens. For one thing, it's cheaper. To have a quarter available in the casino actually costs a quarter. If the casino ever closes, it's an asset that can be cashed in, but in the meantime it's costly to have all that money tied up. On the other hand, it takes only a few cents to have a supplier mint a token with the casino's logo.

The supply of tokens also has to be replenished less frequently than a supply of U.S. coins. Customers will walk out with a few coins in their pocket, meaning the casino's supply of change fluctuates. When tokens are used, most customers will either bet them or cash them in before they leave, keeping the supply of change relatively constant.

Customers walking out the door with a few coins in their pockets lead us to one more reason casinos like tokens. If you have six quarters in your pocket, you might just leave the casino with them. If you have six 25-cent casino tokens, chances are you're going to drop them in the slot instead. Maybe you'll go to the cashier's cage or change booth and get your buck and a half to go home, but the casino knows you're more likely to bet the tokens. Those couple of extra pulls for the road give a little extra padding to the bottom line.

Personally, it doesn't matter to me whether they're coins or tokens—they burn a hole in my pocket. I follow my own advice and play the best games, making the best percentage bets and managing my money carefully. But, when it's time to go, that buck or so in change seems like a small risk.

I date this little weakness back to a Las Vegas trip my wife and I took in 1988. It was our last night, and we had only a couple of hours until it was time to head for the airport. We were playing at Bourbon Street, and Marcy suggested taking a little walk instead of playing right up until time to head back. I was agreeable, but when she headed to the rest room I pulled two quarters out of my pocket and dropped them in a slot. Double bar, double bar, double bar. Forty quarters dropped out of the slot—most machines didn't have credit meters yet in those days.

When Marcy returned, I opened my fist and showed her the 40 quarters. She rolled her eyeballs and led me to a bank of Quarter-mania machines. My first pull I hit for 40 more quarters. On her third, she hit for 20. I hit for another 40, she hit for 100.

In the hour we played, my 50 cents grew to $62.50. A small victory, but we headed home on a winning note.

13. A. Slot manufacturers have been on the rise in recent years, natural enough with the increasing popularity of slots and the dramatic rise in the number of casinos with the legalization of gaming in jurisdictions outside Nevada and New Jersey.

Just a few years ago, nearly every electronic gaming device in the casino was made by IGT or Bally's, with a few from Sigma on the floor. Now Aristocrat, Atronic, WMS, A.C. Coin, Konami, Mikohn and Shuffle Master are players in the field, and more competitors are entering the market all the time.

14. B. Slot machine manufacturers and their products must be licensed by state gaming boards before the company's machines can be placed in casinos. Licensing of the company involves background checks on owners, executives and key employees as well as a look at manufacturing standards and procedures. Licensing a machine involves laboratory tests, making sure it functions properly, lives up to state randomness standards and meets any other state requirements such as minimum and maximum theoretical payback percentages. Sometimes licensing a machine also involves a field test.

15. A. A field test places a new slot machine in a casino or a few casinos on a limited basis. Essentially, it is on trial for a couple of months. Does it function properly? Does it need excessive maintenance? Did the manufacturer get its math right and does the machine pay out within promised limits? The host casino also has an eye on whether the machine is attractive to players. Does it attract business? Even if the machine finally is licensed, the casino is under no obligation to install it permanently if it hasn't proven attractive to customers.

16. B. The majority of slot players play games that have three physical reels and accept two or three coins per play, but the gap is closing. Games on video screens, high-tech games, games with bonuses and games-within-games are carving out an ever-growing share of the casino market.

A look at what IGT has done with its gaming product over the last decade is instructive. When WMS Gaming had the first big video slot hit with Reel 'Em In, and had more video games on the way, IGT, manufacturer of popular games including Red White and Blue, Double Diamonds, Wild Cherry and Five Times Pay, released statistics showing that nine of the 10 most popular slots in the U.S. were IGT machines. And all those games were traditional reel slots.

Still, IGT felt enough pressure that in 1997 it introduced its Vision Series slots, which adapted the game-within-a-game concept to a color LCD screen. Wild Cherry, for example, becomes Wild Cherry Pie. The panel shows a basket of cherries and a pie crust. Each time a Wild Cherry Pie symbol shows in the reel window, regardless of whether it's on the payline, cherries are added to the pie. When the pie is filled, it's gobbled up as a country theme plays. When only crumbs remain, a bonus jackpot is displayed on the pie tin.

By the following year, IGT was showing multiline, multicoin games with video reels and second-screen bonuses. Its video I-Game platform is now one of the most popular in the industry, and video games such as Little Green Men, Lucky Larry's Lobstermania, video versions of *Wheel of Fortune* and many more combine with traditional reel-spinning product to bolster IGT's share of the slot machine market.

17. D. A record jackpot of $39,713,982.25 was hit on a Megabucks machine at Excalibur on the Las Vegas Strip in March 2003. The winner was a 25-year-old software engineer from California who was visiting family in Las Vegas and playing Megabucks at his uncle's suggestion. The jackpot broke the record of $34.9 million at the Desert Inn on the Strip in 2000.

How rapidly things change: When the first edition of this book was published, the record was $27,582,539.48, set in 1998 at Palace Station, west of the Las Vegas Strip. At that time, it nearly doubled the record of $14.4 million set in 1998 at Harrah's in Reno, Nevada. The new record is nearly three times that amount. And the Desert Inn, where the 2000 record was set, is no longer open.

18. C. In the 1950s, slots were the third most popular casino game, well behind craps and blackjack.

The revolution that brought slots to the forefront really started in the 1960s when Bally's developed the coin hopper, first used in that company's Money Honey slots. Until then, coins inside a machine were held in coin tubes, waiting to be paid out. Coin tubes really couldn't hold very many coins, meaning machine-paid payoffs couldn't be very large and machines couldn't accept more than one coin at a time. Take a 10-coin hit and multiply it by two or three coins played, and coin tubes would be drained too rapidly. Multicoin machines would have required too-frequent fills and too-large staffs and would have rendered too-slow service to keep slot players happy. It wasn't until the hopper enabled the slots to circulate coins out of a large pool that multicoin machines really became feasible.

Another key was the advancement from mechanical to electro-mechanical to electronic slots. As we saw in "Reel Spin No. 1: Definitions," mechanical machines couldn't support the huge jackpots that attract players to today's machines. Those had to wait for the computer age.

Once the key pieces were in place—coin hoppers, multicoin games, huge jackpots, electronic slots using computer technology—it didn't take long at all for slot machines to take over the casino world.

19. B. Slot machines are less popular—or at least less numerous—in European casinos.

Traditionally, European casinos were not designed to be for the Everyman or Everywoman. They were for the upper crust, and to bring tourist dollars into the local economy. Even today, many casinos require a player to be a member to be admitted, and membership might require a short waiting period after application. But the casino scene is changing somewhat, and Atronic, with international headquarters in Germany, is a slot leader on the continent. Bally Gaming has a strong presence, too, having brought wide-area progressive jackpots to Russia with its *Playboy* video slots in 2004.

I've mentioned to friends that in England casinos are not allowed to advertise their existence, and the huge neon signs that are part of the casino landscape in the United States are not permitted. If a guidebook promotes an English casino, even without the casino operator's knowledge, the casino's license can be called into question. The reaction from friends, even from friends who have spent considerable time in Great Britain, is invariable: "I didn't even realize there were casinos in England."

Once you're inside, you're not greeted by screaming neon. No signs saying "Up to 98 percent payback!" or "Hottest Slots in Town!" or "Free Pull! Win a New Car!" In fact, usually no slots at all on first glance. The handful of slots are relegated to a separate room, while the main casino houses roulette, baccarat and blackjack.

When the Monte Carlo casino opened on the Las Vegas Strip, much was made of trying to give it a European flavor. I did a walk-through with two friends, one of whom had actually visted Monte Carlo in Monaco. All three of us found a village area with a cobblestone street winding past little shops and a brew pub nicely atmospheric. We walked past a table games pit with a European-style single-zero roulette wheel, and one friend asked the other just how well they had done in creating a European-style casino.

The answer was short: "Too many slots."

20. C. Video slots once had a tough time finding a market, but now are increasing in popularity.

Manufacturers tried to put slot reels on video screens just about as soon as video poker established its popularity in the early 1980s. Players seemed willing to walk miles out of their way, to cross desert without a water bottle, rather than play slots with reels on a video screen. In the late '80s, I once walked through the Flamingo on the Las Vegas Strip on a crowded night. A whole bank of slot machines was mobbed, with onlookers waiting for their chance to play. In the middle of a row, one lonely slot was empty. A video slot.

"Older versions of video reels had poor graphics and poor play characteristics," Dave Hicks, head of slot operations for Harrah's Entertainment in Memphis, told me a while back. "They looked contrived. To the player, they didn't look like a game decided by random luck. Now manufacturers make the player feel like the video screen offers the same actual randomness as a reel game."

The popularity of games like Williams's Reel 'Em In and IGT's I-Games such as Little Green Men and Catch a Wave has changed the way players and operators alike look at the games.

As I was researching a magazine article in mid-1998, I spoke with George Mancuso, vice president of slot operations at the Tropicana in Atlantic City, about the viability of video slots. "The possibilities are endless," he said. "With the bonusing features, we can attract the players with games that are a little bit more fun.

"If there's any trend with regular reel slots it's that fewer will be purchased in the next couple of years. The video games add a lot of entertainment. With multicoin games, you can increase the hit frequency to 40 or 50 percent. They may be small hits, and sometimes the customer doesn't even know why they're being paid, but the next thing they know they're into the second-screen feature."

By increasing the hit frequency to 40 or 50 percent, he means that some video games can be programmed so the player gets some kind of payback on 40 to 50 percent of all pulls. Often, that payback is less than the number of coins wagered. Play 45 coins per spin in IGT's *The Price Is Right* or WMS's Winning Bid sometime, and you'll be amazed at the number of 18- and 36-coin payoffs. It doesn't cover your wager, but it keeps you going and makes you feel like the game is alive while you wait for something bigger and better. That's in stark contrast to traditional three-reel slots, in which almost all payoffs are for several times the size of your bet. To make that work, there have to be many more losing spins than winners.

Is one way better than the other? It's all really a matter of personal preference. Would you rather get a little back on a lot of pulls, or a lot back on just a few pulls interspersed by longer losing streaks? The long-term percentages can be programmed so that they're the same in either style of machine. It's just up to the player to decide which way she'd rather play.

Reel Spin No. 3: Myth and Legends

Can a casino manager really push a jackpot button to reward a long-suffering customer? Are reel-spinners more trustworthy than video slots? The inner workings of slot machines remain a mystery to most players. Just as with most mysterious subjects, widely believed myths and rumors spring up to fill the void left by a lack of solid information. Decide if the following statements about slot machines are True or False:

1. **It is luckier to pull the handle on a slot machine than to hit the "max coins" or "play one coin" button.**
   True
   False

2. **Slots pay more when the player drops coins in by hand instead of playing off the credit meter.**
   True
   False

3. **A machine that has been hot is likely to stay hot.**
   True
   False

4. **A machine that has been ice cold is due to warm up.**
   True
   False

5. A machine that senses warm coins, just paid out as winnings, is less likely to keep paying than if the player uses cool coins.
    True
    False

6. A machine is more likely to pay if the player uses paper money instead of coins.
    True
    False

7. When top jackpot symbols start showing up in the window, but off the payline, a big jackpot is on the way.
    True
    False

8. It's easier for slot manufacturers to manipulate video screens to give low paybacks than to manipulate physical reels.
    True
    False

9. An individual player is more likely to hit a jackpot if the casino is crowded.
    True
    False

10. Casinos rig machines to pay at a higher percentage at night than in the daytime.
    True
    False

11. Casinos rig machines to pay at a higher percentage on week-ends than on weekdays.
    True
    False

12. Casino managers sometimes reward favored players or those who play a long time by pressing a jackpot button, or other-

wise sending a signal from the office to the machine that it's time to pay off.

True

False

13. Slot machines pay off more often if the player bets one coin at a time than if he plays maximum coins.

True

False

14. After hitting a jackpot, it's time to move to another machine because the machine has to make up for the big payout.

True

False

15. If you've played the same machine several days without hitting a jackpot, a big hit is just around the corner.

True

False

16. After a player hits a jackpot, a slot technician opens the machine and flips a switch to lower the payback percentage.

True

False

17. On two otherwise identical-looking slot machines, if one shows a bigger top jackpot, that's the one to play.

True

False

18. If you leave a machine and someone else sits down and hits the jackpot, you'd have been a big winner if you'd just been patient.

True

False

19. **Look for machines not in use in which cherries on the middle reel sit on the payline. They will pay off within the next few pulls.**
    True
    False

20. **Each slot machine has a sequence of results that can be worked out if the customer plays long enough.**
    True
    False

Reel Spin No. 3: Myths and Legends Answers:

1. False. On those slots that still have handles, it is no luckier to pull the handle on a slot machine than to hit the "max coins" or "play one coin" button. In the long run, it makes no difference whether you pull the handle or push the buttons. Your long-term payback percentage will be no different.

The short-term is another matter. Your result for one pull will be different if you pull the handle than if you hit a button. Not necessarily better, and not necessarily worse. Just different. That's because your timing in reaching for the handle will be different than your timing in pushing a button, and timing is everything to the random number generator that determines reel combinations.

In the old days of mechanical slots, some players found it possible to beat certain machines by jerking the handles. Such methods do not help players on today's electronic slots.

Still, I often get letters from readers telling me that when they're in a losing streak while pushing the buttons, they change their luck by pulling the handle. That's fine; it does no harm. But, in the long run, it makes no difference, either.

2. False. Slots do not pay more when the player drops coin in by hand instead of playing off the credit meter. Nor do they pay more when the player plays off the credit meter instead of dropping in coins by hand. The long-term payback is the same. Modern slot machines are programmed so that reel combinations will show up with the same relative frequency regardless of whether you play coins or credits.

3. False. A machine that is hot is no more likely to stay hot than any other machine. In fact, the most likely scenario for a hot machine is that it will cool off.

One reality that slot players have to deal with is that slots are cool a lot more than they're hot. That's the price of offering large potential payoffs for a small investment. Let's say you're playing a machine on which the low end of the pay table is three mixed bars—"three any bars" in casino parlance—that pay you 10 coins for two played. Three single bars pay 20 coins, double bars pay 40, triple bars pay 160 and 7s pay 1,000. Just to balance out three any bars, the machine needs to average four losing spins for every winner. Factor in the other payoffs, and the frequency of winners has to go down still more.

In order to offer large payoffs, slots must have many more losing spins than winners. That leads to short hot streaks and long cool streaks. Even a machine programmed to pay back a high percentage will have long cool streaks.

I once tested a slot machine that a casino manager swore was a 98 percent payback machine. The sign on the bank of machines advertised "98 percent payback!" Not "Up to 98 percent" or any other weasel words that would allow the house to sneak in a low-paying machine next to a high-payer. This individual machine, I was told, was certified at 98 percent. I then had 40 consecutive losing spins.

If you've had a hot streak and want to keep playing the hot machine, I can't blame you. But if that hot machine then gives you 10 losing spins in a row, it's no longer hot and there's no reason to think it's going to warm up again. Continue playing at your own risk.

4. False. A slot machine is never due for anything. Results are as random as humans can program a computer to be. Believing a cold machine is due to warm up, no matter how long you've been playing it, is dangerous.

I once had a phone call from a woman in Illinois asking me to intercede with the gaming board in investigating a machine. She wasn't usually a slot player, she said. She usually played roulette. For her foray into the slots, she chose to play a $5 machine, two coins at a time. She quickly lost the $1,000 she had brought with her. So she took out her credit card, went to the automatic teller machine and took out another thousand. She lost that, and hit up the ATM again. By the time she was done, she had lost more than $8,000, mostly borrowed at credit card interest rates.

"I didn't hit anything," she complained. "I thought that since it had gone so long without paying off, it was due to hit."

Slots are *never* due to hit, and certainly not in the time one player sits at a machine. In Illinois, where this player was gambling, no slot machine may pay off less than 80 percent in the long run, and no machine may pay off more than 100 percent. But the long run is a very long time—100,000 to 300,000 pulls, to meet state standards.

Let's say this woman lost her $8,000 with absolutely no payback. That's not what happened, but I want to make the example extreme. That would mean she played 800 pulls with zero percent payback.

What would the machine have to pay over the next 99,200 pulls to meet the Illinois minimum of 80 percent payback? For a total of 100,000 pulls, during which customers risk $1 million, the machine would have to return $800,000. Compressing that so that the $800,000 payback would all have to come during 99,200 pulls during which time customers risk $992,000, the machine's payback percentage would have to be only 80.6 percent. To reach that particular casino's 96 percent average return on $5 slots, the payback in those remaining 99,200 pulls would have to be only 96.8 percent.

Our player's $8,000 loss is barely a blip on the screen. That's the way slot machines work. Your cold streaks—or hot streaks—in any one gaming session are barely a blip on the screen as far as the casino is concerned. You can't play long enough to reach the point that wins and losses have to begin to balance out.

5. False. Machines are no less likely to pay off if warm coins rather than cool coins are used. I thought this particular myth had died out years ago, but I was asked this very question at a seminar I gave in 1998. Then, when I gave a talk to a senior citizens' group in 2001, well after the original edition of this book was printed, the same question came up again. Old legends die hard, it seems, but slot machines have no heat sensors that would enable them to detect hot vs. cold coins. They don't know if the coins you play come from your pocket, the change person or their own hoppers.

6. False. The machine is no more likely to pay off if you use paper money instead of coins.

The random number generator, the computer program that determines what combinations are going to come up on the reels, doesn't know if you're playing with coins or paper money, or whether you're playing credits or dropping in one coin at a time. The RNG is on a separate computer chip from the program that counts your money.

Nevertheless, I used to recommend to players on short bankrolls that they play coins instead of credits. Even if they start by sliding currency into the bill validator, I suggest that they then cash out and feed the coins back into the slot.

Why? Because play is slower when you use coins. Before bill validators, the casino used to assume customers played about 240 pulls per hour. Now some play 400, 500 even 600 pulls per hour, and it's possible to play as many as 1,000 pulls per hour if you're hitting the "max coins" button just as fast as the reels come to a stop.

Drop coins in by hand, and you slow down play and lessen your risk by limiting the number of wagers. Some slot players find that boring. Others with limited funds find it a good way to make their money last on their day at the casino.

That piece of advice is on its way to becoming obsolete as casinos switch over to making payoffs with ticket printers. Some machines, especially at low denominations, have no slots in which to drop the coins. Besides, if you're playing a penny slot with a

200-coin maximum bet, who's going to drop in all those coins? That would be slow play indeed.

7. False. Having jackpot symbols turn up off the payline decidedly does not mean a big hit's on the way. It's just another losing spin. Smart players take it that way. No matter how pretty they look in the window, losing spins have no effect on upcoming plays.

A while back a television report accused slot manufacturers of programming machines so that winning symbols turned up frequently in the slot window but off the payline in order to sucker players into thinking a winner was coming. Now, it's possible that some programs do result in jackpot symbols showing up more frequently just above and just below the payline than the player would expect, but that can be a natural outgrowth of programming that allows bigger jackpots than the physical reels would support.

But, regardless of how or why it's done, it doesn't matter how often jackpot symbols turn up off the payline. I repeat: *it doesn't matter.* The TV report was much ado about very little. The only symbols that matter are those that land on the payline. If they land anywhere else, in or out of the player's view, it's just another losing spin. Ignore the losers and move on.

8. False. It is no easier to manipulate results on video screens than on physical reels. Nowadays video slots and reel-spinners are programmed in much the same way. The reels are just a representation of a mathematical game that's being played by the computer in the machine's core.

In fact, if the electronic record of a spin and what shows on the reels differ, casinos can and will allow the electronic record to supersede the reels. Often, in the case of large hand-paid jackpots, the electronic record must be verified before the jackpot is paid. Some state laws even bar the casino from paying a jackpot if the electronic record doesn't match what shows on the reels.

In part, that's an anti-cheating regulation. A player who finds a way to manipulate the reels would also have to find a way to manipulate the electronic record before stealing a jackpot—and that's a tall order. Also, in states that expect gaming to be a cash cow and impose gaming taxes that range up to 70 percent of casino revenue, with no deductions for expenses, the states are going to make darn sure a jackpot is fairly won before taking the hit on their own bottom lines.

9. False. An individual player is no more likely to hit a jackpot if the casino is crowded. I once read a book in which the author advised slot players to play at peak times in busy casinos, because that's when the most jackpots are hit. And it's true. More jackpots are hit at peak times in busy casinos than when the casinos aren't so busy.

Why? Because more machines are played more often at peak times. How does that affect my chances of hitting? Not at all.

Let's say I'm in a casino with 1,000 slot machines, each programmed to pay off the top jackpot about once per 20,000 pulls. It's Saturday night, so every machine is busy, all with steady players spinning the reels at about 500 pulls per hour. In two hours, the reels spin a collective 1 million times and, if the machines hit right on the average, 50 jackpots are paid. One in every 20 players has a big payday. If I'm not one of them, I've at least seen a few jackpots paid.

Now let's say I return early Wednesday morning. Only 100 slot players are in the casino, playing the same 500 pulls per hour as those on the busier night. In two hours, the reels spin only 100,000 times, only 10 percent as much as on the busy night. If the machines hit right on the average, only five jackpots are paid.

Fifty jackpots on the busy night. Five on the slow day.

But with only 100 players in the casino, those five jackpots mean one in every 20 players has a big payday—the same as on the busy night. My chances of being one of those to hit the jackpot are the same on the calm day as on the busy night.

10. False. I once had a reader write to me to complain that casinos loosen the machines in the daytime so the idle rich get all the jackpots, then tighten them at night so that the good stuff isn't available to working people. It just isn't so.

The flip side is a complaint I once received from a senior citizen, claiming that machines were tight in the daytime when retirees make up a large percentage of customers, and looser at night for the younger folk after work.

Casinos do not rig machines to pay at a higher percentage in the daytime than at night or higher at night than in daytime. Nor is the operation simple enough to routinely do such a thing if the operator wanted to. In many gaming states, the computer chip holding the random number generator must be sealed by evidence tape. If the casino decides to change the payback percentage by changing the chip, a gaming board agent must be present to watch the evidence tape being broken and the chip sealed with new evidence tape.

11. False. Just as casinos do not change the payback percentages from day to night, they do not change them from weekdays to weekends. If it seems you see more jackpots hit on weekends, just remember that more people are playing, meaning there are more random chances for a jackpot to turn up.

12. False. There is no remote jackpot button by which casino managers reward favored players. If you hit a jackpot, it's because the random number generator has generated a jackpot combination at the very instant you drop a coin in the slot, hit the "bet one" button or hit the "max coins" button. No one is out there rigging a jackpot because they like you, nor are they taking pity on you. Every player is simply taking his chances with the RNG.

13. False. Slots do not pay off more often if the player bets one coin at a time than if he plays maximum coins. This might be the most common myth among slot players today. I find myself forced to answer this question in my newspaper column two or three times a year, and it seems that as soon as I answer it I get another sheaf of letters asking the same question. Often they start, "I've never seen this question answered before, but I've always wondered if the slot machines are fixed to pay off more often when you only bet one coin."

They aren't, and they don't. The random number generator doesn't even know how many coins you've played. The counting and paying programs are on a different chip. All the RNG does is generate numbers corresponding to reel combinations, and it fixes a combination for the upcoming pull as soon as it receives a signal that you're actually going to play—when you drop the first coin in the slot, when you hit the "bet one" button or when you hit the "max bet" button. The number of coins you then play does not affect the number being generated or the reel combination that will land on the payline.

14. False. After a machine has paid a big jackpot, it has no immediate need to make up for the big payout. The likelihood of hot and cold streaks is exactly the same as before you hit the jackpot. The likelihood of your hitting the jackpot again on the next pull is even the same as it was before your big hit. Slot machine results are as random as humans can program them to be. The programmed percentages will hold up over a very long time, but in the short term a slot can just as easily pay 10 percent, 50 percent or 200 percent of its average long-term return. That's just as true immediately after a jackpot as before.

15. False. If you've played the same machine for days without hitting a jackpot, it doesn't mean one is around the corner. In fact, the odds of your hitting the jackpot are the same as when you started. That's part of what we mean when we say results are random. If the chances of a jackpot combination landing on the payline are 1 in 20,000, they're 1 in 20,000 on your first pull, 1 in 20,000 on your 1,000th pull and 1 in 20,000 on your 20,000th pull. The random number generator is just as likely to generate the jackpot number at one time as at any other.

Nevertheless, most players won't play a machine on which a jackpot combination is showing, believing that it's going to be a long time before the next jackpot turns up. That's why casino employees always ask the player to spin the reels again after a hand-paid jackpot. The casino doesn't want the winning combination to show and keep others away from the machine.

16. False. After a jackpot is hit, the slot technician does not open the machine to flip a switch and lower the payback percentage. He might open the machine to verify that the combination that shows on the reels matches the electronic outcome of the pull. That does not mean he's changing the payback percentage. Slot manufacturers and casino operators know the top jackpot is going to be hit once in a while, and they know about how often it's going to hit. That's already accounted for in the programmed payback percentage. There is no need for the casino to drive the percentage lower to make up ground faster after a big hit. In the long run—and the casinos are in it for the long run—jackpots are just a normal part of play.

17. False—or at least not necessarily. If one machine has a bigger top jackpot than the other of two otherwise identical-looking slot machines, it does not necessarily mean the one with the bigger prize has a bigger payback percentage. The machine with a lesser jackpot could be programmed so that paybacks occur more frequently, and could have a higher overall payback than the machine with the bigger prize. There is no way to tell by looking at the machines.

18. False. If someone else hits the jackpot on a machine you just left, it does not mean you'd have been a big winner if you'd just been patient. For you to have had the same results as your replacement, you'd have needed the same exact time, to the split second. If you were a microsecond faster or slower to drop a coin or hit the button, you'd have had a different outcome.

Any change in timing will change your result on the individual spin. If you say hello to another player just sitting down, or take a drink, or see where that loud cheer is coming from, or give an order to the cocktail waitress, the outcome of your next pull will be different than if you'd just kept playing. There's no way to tell what your outcome would have been. But you can be pretty sure that the results would have been different if someone else were sitting in your place.

19. False. This is an oddball myth I read in a financial newsletter, of all places. It's a good newsletter, with some excellent tips. This isn't one of them. It is not true that cherries sitting on the payline of the middle reel mean that a win is coming up. The random number generator runs continuously, even when nobody is playing the machine. One pull has no influence on the next. And the combination that shows on the reels as you approach the screen has absolutely no effect on what's to come.

20. False—and that makes it a clean sweep, with 20 myths and 20 answers of "false." There is no discernable pattern to slot machine results. Results are as random as humans can program a computer to be. Even if there was, no one can observe long enough to map out a pattern. How long would you have to play, for instance, to find a pattern for Megabucks, with its multimillion-dollar jackpots? Any non-random sequence would have to be billions of numbers long, given that the Nevada Megabucks system sometimes goes years at a time without paying off the top jackpot, even with dozens of casinos throughout the state participating.

A slot player brought this up at a seminar I once gave. She said that, for several spins in a row, she and the player next to her had the exact same reel combinations. She'd wondered if just for a few spins they were in sync, that they had reached the same place in the machine's pattern.

What was at work here was simply random chance, one of the oddball things that happen when you're dealing with such impossibly large numbers as the number of times handles are pulled or buttons pushed on slot machines. Players send the reels spinning more than a trillion times a month, and given enough trials anything that possibly can happen eventually will.

That includes two people on adjacent machines having the same results for several spins. If the question is, "Will this happen to me today," it's an extreme long shot. If the question is, "Will this happen to someone at some time," it's a certainty.

Reel Spin No. 4: A Slot Potpourri

What does it mean when there's a coin cup on the top of a slant-top slot machine screen? Is it okay to play more than one machine at a time? Do casinos place high-paying machines in certain areas? Who invented slot machines, anyway?

See if you can provide the answers to this collection of slot etiquette, lore and trivia:

1. **A coin cup atop the video screen or reel window of a slant-top slot machine means:**
    A. The machine is out of order.
    B. The machine is occupied by a player taking a break.
    C. The machine is out of coins and needs a hopper fill.

2. **Playing more than one machine at a time:**
    A. Narrows the house edge.
    B. Ensures the player of finding at least one loose machine.
    C. Costs the player more money in the long run.

3. **Playing more than one machine at a time:**
    A. Is sometimes limited by casinos in crowded periods.
    B. Is banned outright by some casinos.
    C. Is always tolerated and even encouraged.

4. **A customer who wants to drop coins into the slot may exchange currency for rolls of coins from:**
   A. A change person, who pushes a change cart on wheels.
   B. A change booth.
   C. The cashier's cage.
   D. Any of the above.
   E. None of the above.

5. **A customer can cash in his or her coins or tokens for currency:**
   A. With a change person.
   B. At a change booth.
   C. At the cashier's cage.
   D. Any of the above.
   E. None of the above.

6. **If a change person or other casino employee directs the player to a specific machine, the customer should:**
   A. Grab that machine while it's hot.
   B. Thank the employee for the advice and choose his own machine.
   C. Run for the exits.

7. **It is customary to tip the change person:**
   A. Any time you buy change or cash in.
   B. When you hit a hand-paid jackpot.
   C. When she calls someone to fill the hopper.

8. **Jackpots are paid by hand:**
   A. Whenever they're over $500.
   B. Whenever they're over $1,000.
   C. Whenever they're too big for the coin capacity of the hopper.

9. **Casinos usually place their highest-paying machines:**
   A. Near table games.
   B. At the ends of rows.
   C. Near the elevators.
   D. None of the above.

10. Slot machines have been in existence for about:
   A. 50 years.
   B. 100 years.
   C. 200 years.
   D. 500 years.

11. The first recognizably modern 3-reel slot machine was:
   A. The Statue of Liberty.
   B. The Liberty Bell.
   C. The Capitol.
   D. The Minuteman.

12. The first three-reel slot was invented by:
   A. Charles Fey.
   B. Martha Raye.
   C. Doris Day.
   D. Danny Kaye.

13. Instead of cash, early slot machines sometimes paid in:
   A. Golf balls.
   B. Chewing gum.
   C. Cigars.
   D. All of the above.

14. Orange, plum and lemon symbols, all still used on slot machines today, were introduced on slot machines to signify:
   A. The inventor's roots as a fruit-stand vendor.
   B. Flavors of chewing gum.
   C. Wealth, as fresh fruit then was so expensive.
   D. None of the above.

15. The black horizontal line "bar" symbols now common on slot machine reels are derived from:
   A. A logo for the taverns and bars that once were the most common homes for slot machines.
   B. A logo for a group that tried to have the machines barred in Nevada.
   C. A logo for a chewing gum company.
   D. None of the above.

Reel Spin No. 4: A Slot Potpourri Answers

1. B. A coin cup on top of a video screen or reel window on a slant-top slot machine is occupied by a player taking a break. It used to be common to leave the cups over the slot handles. Now, of course, handles are an endangered species, and even coin cups will disappear once all machines have changed over to payouts by ticket printers or smart cards.

Other signals used by players include leaving jackets or sweaters on chairs or stools by the machines, or leaving drinks or cigarettes on the machines themselves. I've even seen players leave personal belongings, including wallets and purses, on machines. That, of course, is unwise, and an invitation to theft.

It's okay to take breaks during play and expect your machine to be waiting for you when you get back. Just be sure the breaks are of reasonable length. Reserving a machine while you go to the bathroom, find the change person or get a drink is reasonable. Saving a machine while you go play a different game for a while or take a nap is not. Some casinos will even save the machine for you while you take a dinner break—just ask a slot host. That's fine in a large casino with plenty of places to play, but it's less than considerate on a crowded riverboat with limited gaming options. In crowded conditions, try to keep your breaks short, or else pick up your belongings and accept that you'll have to find somewhere else to play after a longer break.

2. C. Playing more than one machine costs the player more money in the long run. Many players think that, of two machines placed side-by-side, one is bound to be hot. That is not necessarily the case—and, even if it were, playing two machines would still lead to bigger long-term losses than playing one. That's because even on "loose" machines the casino still has an edge. Not only that, a customer can play each of two machines nearly as fast as playing just one by pushing one machine's buttons while reels are spinning on the other. That doubles the risk.

Let's say I've found two two-coin $1 machines sitting side by side. By chance, I've hit it lucky—one of my machines is a red-hot 98 percent payback slot; the other returns an average 95 percent in the long run. (I can't really tell from the outside what the payback percentages are; we're trusting dumb luck here.)

If I just play the 95 percenter for an hour at 500 spins per hour, I risk $1,000 and on the average lose $50. But let's say I play both machines at a slightly slower 400 spins per hour instead. Now on the 95 percenter I risk $800 per hour and on the average lose $40. On the 98 percenter I risk $800 and lose $16. My total losses rise to $56 per hour—more than if I'd just stayed with the weaker machine.

And that's if I hit it lucky and hit upon a high-paying machine. What if I've found two average machines? Now I've doubled my risk without increasing the rewards on either. What if one of them is an ice-cold 85 percenter? Ouch!

Still, many players like going after more than one machine at a time. Maybe they find making another bet more entertaining than watching the results of the first machine. To them, I'd just add a caution to watch out for theft. If you're watching two machines, it's more difficult to keep an eye on purses and personal belongings. I once saw a woman playing a whole row of eight machines— pushing buttons in sequence, walking back and forth and forth and back. When she was playing at one end, she was vulnerable to theft at the other. Be wary.

3. A. Playing more than one machine is sometimes limited in crowded casinos. On my regular rounds, several casinos have signs at machines asking players to limit themselves to one machine when the casino is crowded. If the casino lets the player in the door—especially on board riverboats with limited gaming positions—they are under an obligation to provide that customer a place to play. That sometimes means restricting players to one machine at a time.

4. D. The player can make change with a change person, at a change booth or at the cashier's cage. Or the player can circumvent the whole process by sliding currency into the bill validator of the machine he's about to play, then push the cash-out button and play the change.

Employees pushing change carts around the slot floor used to be a standard part of casino operations. The advent of bill validators and playing off credit meters instead of dropping coins one by one greatly reduced the need for change and change people, and ticket printers soon will relegate change carts to antique status. But, as long as there are machines with coin heads, there will be players who prefer to drop the coins into the slots, and limited change service is needed for those players.

5. D. With some restrictions, the player can cash in coins or tokens with a change person, at a change booth or at the cashier's cage.

In large casinos that have both cashier's cages and change booths, coin transactions might be limited to the change booths. Sometimes both have coin counters that enable the casino to swiftly exchange coins or tokens for currency. But sometimes the cashier's cage is restricted to exchanges of gaming chips from the tables plus paper transactions such as cashing checks or taking credit. When that's the case, you'll be sent to a change booth to cash in your coins. As a rule of thumb, if you see separate change booths, use them to exchange coins or tokens for currency.

The few remaining people wheeling the change carts some-times will buy back large denomination tokens from players. They do not have coin counters, and they won't take your quarters or nickels, but, if you rack up your $1, $2 or $5 tokens in racks holding 100 tokens each, they can give you cash. Even in 2002, after I hit a 400-coin jackpot on a $2 machine at the Tropicana in Las Vegas, a woman pushing a change cart handed me racks for the tokens, then gave me cash for the filled racks.

6. B. Be polite, but if a casino employee recommends a machine the decision is still up to you. Change persons are not privy to data on what chip is in what machine, or what machines have the highest payback percentages. If they point out a machine of the type you would play anyway, there's no harm in trying, but they don't have access to such solid information that you should change your pattern of play on their say-so.

Of course, there are times to head straight for the exits, too. One of them is when an employee loudly and insistently tries to steer you toward a machine.

Once, I was showing an old friend from Colorado the sights of downtown Las Vegas. We came across a small, all-slots casino, with someone outside handing out bonus coupons. "Let's check this out," Scott said.

I just grinned. I knew what was coming.

As we entered, a woman wearing a casino name badge rushed to greet us.

"Dollars! Dollars! Dollars!" she shouted. "You fellows play dollars?"

Scott said yes, even though I hadn't seen him play many dol-lars in the last couple of days.

She started in again.

"This machine! This machine! Play this one! This is the lucky one! You here!"

We didn't even have a chance to walk through and see what was there. And we were seated at dollar machines.

"All right! It's double jackpot time for dollar players! Hit a hand-paid jackpot and you're paid double! Double! Double! Double! Go! Go! Go!"

I kept my wallet in my pants and looked at Scott. He kept his wallet in his pants and looked at me. And he burst out laughing—he'd figured it all out.

"We *don't* have to do this," he said, shaking his head.

"No, we don't," I agreed.

"Let's get out of here," he grinned.

And as we left, the woman who had been so enthused looked at us sheepishly and said, "Sorry, guys."

That's a game that's played in some all-slots casinos every day. There's a hard sell outside the door to get you in, and then another hard sell to guide you to specific machines. Guide enough players to enough machines, and eventually someone will hit a jackpot—and perhaps give a big tip.

7. B. Many players will tip the slot attendant who calls in their hand-paid jackpot. Many also tip the security guard who oversees the payoff, and some will even tip the slot supervisor. It's up to you—entirely voluntary.

Those of you who have hit $1,000 jackpots—a pretty common hand-pay—will note that they're often paid in nine $100 bills and five $20 bills. The hope is that the smaller bills will whisper "Tip" to the player. Tipping $20 on a $1,000 payoff is generous. So is $10 or even $5, especially if you're tipping more than one person.

The advent of machines that take dozens or hundreds of coins at a time has made hand-pays more common, at least until ticket printers take over. The machine glass will often say something like, "Machine pays up to 1,000 coins," or some other amount. Once you exceed that figure on the credit meter, hitting the cash out button will bring a hand-pay. In such cases, a hand-pay doesn't mean you've hit a jackpot. You may even have lost money for the session. On a nickel machine taking 45 coins at a time—$2.25 per pull—a maximum-coin better might start with a $100 bill, just as on a dollar three-reel machine. That's 2,000 nickels. If the player then chooses to cash out 1,600 credits, it means he or she has lost 400 nickels, or $20. The hand-pay is no jackpot payoff, and most players won't tip in that situation.

8. C. Jackpots are paid by hand when they're too big for the capacity of the hopper. On both quarter and nickel machines, I've had the hopper spit out as many as 2,000 coins, which I then had to take to a change booth to get currency. On the other hand, on dollar machines with their larger tokens taking up more hopper space, I've had hand-pays as small as $400.

We tend to think of hand-paid jackpots as being large sums, the kind of hits that will guarantee us coming home with a profit. But I've had hand-pays of less than $20 on some of the new 100-coin penny slots. Of course, $20 amounts to 2,000 pennies, a bit much for the machine to process.

In addition, really big wins are always paid by hand, regardless of hopper capacity. The IRS requires the casino to have the player sign form W2-G before paying one-spin winnings of $1,200 or more.

9. D. Neither near table games, at the ends of rows nor near the elevators are places you're particularly likely to find high-paying slots. That the big payers are at the ends of rows is one of the most enduring rumors in casino lore. A casino slot director once told me that particular myth is so widespread that he had taken to placing weak-paying machines at the ends of rows. He figured he'd get extra play on low-paying machines since so many players would gravitate to that location.

In his outstanding book *Break the One-Armed Bandits*, Frank Scoblete interviewed a casino executive he called "Mr. Handle" on placement of slots. Mr. Handle told Frank to look for machines that were widely visible, that players could see from a variety of angles. Then everyone would be sure to see the fellow players winning, and perhaps would take up positions at lower-paying machines.

Shortly after the book came out, I was walking through Circus Circus, on a wide walkway leading from one gaming area to another. There I saw it. The machine that was visible from every angle, the one that everyone who passed through this walkway would see, regardless of what direction they were walking.

I had two quarters in my pocket—not enough for a fair test at all. I dropped them in the slot. Bam! Bam! Bam! Triple Bar! Triple Bar! Triple Bar! One hundred and sixty quarters came pouring into the tray. I scooped them into a cup and continued on my way.

Evidence of a winning formula? No, this was nowhere near a serious test. It was just random chance, a one-time freak pull. But I gave Frank a hearty "Thanks!" the next time I saw him.

10. B. Slot machines have been around for a little more than 100 years. Some of the most popular early devices didn't look much like our modern idea of a slot machine—they accepted and paid out coins, but instead of reels the machines had large revolving wheels divided into color segments. On the machines developed by Gustav Schultze in San Francisco, players wagered on what color would stop on the indicator. Other popular early machines were based on five-card poker, although these typically did not pay out coins. Payoffs had to come from the operator.

11. B. The Liberty Bell, completed in 1899 in San Francisco, was the first recognizably modern three-reel slot. Reel symbols included horseshoes, stars, spades, diamonds, hearts and bells. It was so popular that for a time all three-reel slots were referred to as "bell machines." With a casing made of sheet metal on a brass frame, it was durable and attractive. There was no neon, flashing lights or sound effects, but show any casino player a Liberty Bell today and they'd recognize it instantly as an antique slot machine, played by dropping a coin in the slot and pulling the handle, just as players have been doing for a century.

12. A. Charles Fey invented the Liberty Bell, and a whole series of machines that included the Horseshoe, with symbols of stars and horseshoes on a wheel, and the Card Bell, an early cash-paying poker machine. A German immigrant with a background making instruments for electrical supply companies, Fey set up a workshop in his basement in Berkeley. It was there that he created many early slot machines.

For a fascinating look at the life of Charles Fey and the development of early slot machines, I refer you to *Slot Machines: A Pictorial History of the First 100 Years.* The lavishly illustrated book was compiled by Charles Fey's grandson, Marshall Fey.

13. D. Many early slots were used as trade stimulators by merchants, and paid out golf balls, chewing gum, candy, cigars and more. A frequent prize was free drinks. Some versions of the Liberty Bell listed a pay table with a top jackpot of 20 free drinks for three bells. Some poker machines paid as many as 100 free drinks for a royal flush. Of course, if a little cash changed hands instead of free drinks, that was between the customer and the merchant.

14. B. The fruit symbols still used on slot machines today come to us from flavors of chewing gum dispensed by the Liberty Bell Gum Fruit slot made by Herbert Mills in Chicago in 1910. Not all the gum symbols survived to modern slot machine use—we see no current machines that use spearmint leaves as a reel symbol.

15. C. The bar symbol commonly used on today's slot machine is identical to the Bell Fruit Gum logo used as a symbol used on early slot machines. The only difference is that nowadays the white lettering on the black bar says "BAR," whereas it used to say "BELL FRUIT GUM."

The bar also bears more than a passing resemblance to the Wrigley arrow still used on packages of Spearmint and Doublemint gum. Some early slot machines dispensing Wrigley's gum used the Wrigley arrow as a symbol.

Reel Spin No. 5: Know Your Machine

When we walk into casinos, we're confronted with hundreds, even thousands of glitzy slot machines all shouting, "Play me!" with their flashing lights and alluring sounds. Some spin the reels just as slot machines have for a century; others use live-action video, special effects and high-fidelity sound.

Can you tell who makes your favorite machine at a glance? And is what you see what you get in the new bonusing games? Try matching up 10 manufacturers with the games they make, then see if you can match the machine to the bonus it offers.

KNOW THE MANUFACTURER

Match the slot machine manufacturer with its signature games:

1. **IGT**
2. **WMS**
3. **Shuffle Master**
4. **Sigma**
5. **Aristocrat**
6. **Bally's**
7. **Atronic**
8. **A.C. Coin**
9. **Konami**
10. **Mikohn**

A. Reel-spinning slots with bonus features in the top box, such as Treasure Tunnel and Treasure Wheel; multiline video slots that include the popular Game of Life series, along with Where's Henry games, themed gamed including Big Mouth Billy Bass and PBR (Professional Bull Riders); Easy Riches video slots on which every payline qualifies for a progressive jackpot.

B. Video slots with second-screen bonuses, such as Reel 'Em In, Cash Crop, Winning Bid and Jackpot Party; reel-spinning slots, often with orange Dotmation screens for bonus rounds, such as Mermaid's Gold, Big Bank Piggy Bankin' and reel-spinning Jackpot Party; licensed theme games such as Monopoly, Pac-Man, *Hollywood Squares* and *Survivor.*

C. Slotto games with a reel-spinning base and bonus rounds using lottery balls in the top box; other slots with innovative use of top box bonuses, such as Hot Diggity Dog and Little Green Men Jr.; video slots with top box bonuses, such as video Slotto and the barbecue-themed King of the Grill.

D. Australian-style video games and reel-spinners with multiple paylines, scatter awards, free spins and first-screen bonuses, including Queen of the Nile, Penguin Pays, Storm Chaser and Tiki Torch; Hyperlink progressive jackpot system with a four-way progressive jackpot.

E. Lots of everything. Traditional three-reel slots such as Red White and Blue, Double Diamonds, Five Times Pay, Wild Cherry; big wide-area progressive jackpots, as in Megabucks and Quartermania; pop-culture-themed slots, as in *Wheel of Fortune, Jeopardy!, I Love Lucy,* Austin Powers and Elvis; video slots with and without pop culture ties, as in Little Green Men, Lucky Larry's Lobstermania, Uncle Sam, *The Munsters, M*A*S*H, Star Wars* and *Dilbert.*

F. Unusual hybrid slots with video bonus rounds on a screen not visible during regular play, such as Ninja vs. Ninja; bonus slots both on video and reel formats such as Show

Me the Mummy; multiplayer slots with a huge center display for bonus play, such as Fortune Orb.

G. Multiline video slots with bonus rounds that reward player skill or knowledge, as in Clue, Trivial Pursuit, *Ripley's Believe It or Not,* Battleship and Yahtzee; reel-spinning slots with pachinko-style bonus games in the top box, as in Liberty Ball and Kazoingo.

H. Reel-spinning slots, multiline video slots with bonuses and hybrid slots with a reel-spinning base game and video screen in the top box for bonus rounds; licensed characters galore, with Betty Boop, Popeye, Blondie and the *Saturday Night Live* gang; Cash for Life progressive slot system in which players can win $1,000 a week or more for the rest of their lives; the Game Maker, the first unit on which players could choose among several screens by touching an on-screen icon.

I. Multiline video slots with bonus rounds, mostly based on pop culture themes such as *Press Your Luck, Let's Make a Deal,* the Three Stooges, *The Amazing Spider-Man* and Sidney Omarr's Horoscope.

J. High-resolution video games with multiple paylines and second-screen bonus rounds and first-screen bonuses, including Sphinx, Babooshka, Clowning Around and Atlantica; wide-area progressives with a video game at the base and a bonus round that uses flip cards in the top box, such as Sphinx Gold and Xanadu.

KNOW THE MACHINE

There are hundreds of different slot games on casino floors at any given time. Let's take a small sampling, and try to match the bonus with its game:

1. **Dilbert's Wheelbert**

2. **Big Mouth Billy Bass**

3. *Wheel of Fortune*

4. *Survivor*

5. **Elvis**

6. **Hot Diggity Dog**

7. *Chicago*

8. *Men in Black*

9. **Wink Martindale's Survey of America**

10. *Saturday Night Live:* **The Coneheads**

A. The basic game is a reel-spinner decorated to look like an old-time hot dog wagon. Up top are two rows of five hot dogs wearing bow ties and smiles. When a special symbol lands on the payline, the hot dogs rise and sit in time to the music, and the player can see each red hot wears a bonus amount that can't been seen when the franks are at rest. The last one standing reveals the bonus for that round.

B. The basic game is a reel-spinner. A "Spin the Wheel" lands on the payline and game show noises begin and a button lights up. The player pushes the button and a wheel showing bonus amounts spins atop the machine. Wherever the wheel stops, the indicated bonus is added to the credit meter.

C. The basic game is a video slot. In one bonus round, the player is asked to guess how many people in a survey of 100 gave a specific answer—for example, how many people among 100 surveyed said they could whistle? The closer the player comes to the answer, the higher the bonus.

D. The basic game is a video slot. In one of several second-screen bonuses, the player is taken to a courtroom, and must find the one juror who thinks the defendant is not guilty. When that juror is found, the defendant tap dances out of court, leaving a bonus behind.

E. The basic game is a reel-spinner. The top box has a video screen for a bonus round in which the player picks an animated contestant to perform tasks involving skills needed to survive in the wild. Cabinet graphics include jungle foliage and a waterfall.

F. The basic game is a video reel slot. In one bonus round, the player chooses a character to toss rings over the top of another character's head, with rings that stay on building the bonus.

G. The basic game is a video reel slot. When the player hits three wordless panels from a *Dilbert* cartoon, the player touches the screen to choose a panel that will reveal the bonus. All three panels are enlarged, and the words are filled in, both in sight and sound, before the reward is revealed.

H. The basic game is a video reel slot. When the three top-secret folders line up, a second screen shows the player 20 confidential files. Most contain bonus amounts, and the player touches files to accumulate bonuses. When a file instead has a picture of an alien, another screen is launched with five human-looking folks in the park. The player tries to touch the character who really is an alien. An x-ray is taken, and a correct guess brings the biggest bonus.

I. The basic game is a reel-spinner. When the player hits a gold record on the payline, the player presses a lighted button. A blinking light flashes around a circle of 14 hit records. When the light stops, that song is played, with concert footage on an LCD panel, which then reveals the player's bonus award.

J. The basic game is a video slot. When three fish on plaques land on the screen, the player goes fishing, selects a lure and sees which fish gets snagged. After a fish is caught, values of lure and fish are revealed and multiplied to yield a bonus.

Reel Spin No. 5: Know Your Machine Answers

KNOW THE MANUFACTURER

1. E. IGT is the largest slot manufacturer in the world. It made its name in the early 1980s as the dominant maker of video poker machines, and before long surpassed Bally Gaming as No. 1 in reel slots with popular favorites such as Red White and Blue, Wild Cherry and Double Diamond. When video slots began to make inroads in the market in the late 1990s, IGT adapted quickly with its "I-Game" series of video slots, including Fortune Cookie, where players build bonuses by choosing dishes from a Chinese menu; the outer-space-themed Little Green Men; and Lucky Larry's Lobstermania. Perhaps the biggest IGT hit of the late 1990s and the early years of the new millennium was *Wheel of Fortune,* which incorporates graphics and sound of the TV show in both reel-spinning and video versions. The success of *Wheel of Fortune* was a precursor to many other pop culture–themed slot machines, including *I Love Lucy, Jeopardy!, The Price Is Right, M*A*S*H, Laverne and Shirley, The Addams Family, The Munsters* and many more. IGT also is king of the wide-area progressives, linking machines in different casinos to build huge jackpots, as in the multimillion-dollar game Megabucks.

2. B. WMS Gaming started as Williams, a division of the company that makes arcade games under the Williams, Gottlieb and Bally's names. The gaming division has since been spun off into its own company. It was through WMS that video slot machines made their big breakthrough in the United States. Inspired by the overseas success of Australian manufacturers such as Aristocrat, and under duress because courts had ruled WMS's reel-spinning games violated patents held by IGT, WMS introduced its first multicoin, multi-line video slot, Reel 'Em In, which uses scatter pays and second-screen bonuses. The success of Reel 'Em In opened the eyes of other slot manufacturers, who soon followed with video slots of their own. WMS firmed up a place as a video leader with fun, creative games including a video version of the reel-spinning hit Jackpot Party, some musical fun with Off the Charts and the farm-fresh, multi-tiered bonuses of Cash Crop, where the player has a chance to grow several "crops" onscreen for big rewards. WMS also produces reel-spinning slots, having secured appropriate licenses from IGT, and has licensed pop culture icons for games that include reel-spinning and video versions of Monopoly, the reel-spinning *Survivor,* and video slots *Hollywood Squares,* Pac-Man and *Men in Black.* Always strong on graphics and characters, WMS stepped forward several notches in 2003 with the introduction of its CPU-NXT game platform, with high resolution and film-quality animation, and its ergonomically designed Bluebird slot cabinet.

3. I. Shuffle Master is unusual among slotmakers in that its entry into the casino market was as a manufacturer of shuffling machines used at table games. That's still a major segment of Shuffle Master's business. It also distributes table games such as Let It Ride and Three Card Poker. In the late 1990s, Shuffle Master entered the slot arena with the reel-spinning Three Stooges game, in partnership with IGT. Partnering with the much larger IGT has worked well for Shuffle Master on video games such as *The Honeymooners* and *Let's Make a Deal.* One unusual video slot is Budweiser, with a cabinet shaped like a beer bottle. One second-screen bonus is built around Bud's series of commercials starring the lizards, Louie and Frank. As the player touches on-screen hiding places, trying to find swamp creatures for bonuses, the lizards provide commentary. When I tested the game, Louie claimed that "When they win, I win," and encouraged players to send him a check, leading to this exchange:

FRANK: Easy, Louie. No one's sending you any money.
LOUIE: Why not?
FRANK: You don't have a bank account.

4. A. Sigma is licensed in every gaming state in the United States, and competes in just about every market segment with video poker, video reel and reel-spinning slots. It was one of the first companies to put a bonus system in the top box of its Treasure Tunnel, with a series of lighted circles, narrowing into a tunnel, that gives the player a chance to multiply a jackpot. The tunnel lights flash off and on in sequence, and the last one lit is the player's multiplier. Sigma has produced some very innovative games, including Big Top Circus, in which the player bets on symbols instead of paylines. The Where's Henry? series includes several video slots in which the player tries to locate the Henry character in a second-screen bonus round. The Game of Life, a joint venture with Harrah's Entertainment, has been a big hit, with a third game in the series, Life Around the World, having come out in 2003. Other licensed games include Big Mouth Billy Bass, incorporating the wisecracking fish in the top box, and PBR, a Professional Bull Riders–themed game that counts trying to have your rider stay astride a bull among its animated bonus rounds.

5. D. Aristocrat makes both reel-spinning and video games, but really excels at multiple-payline games with scatter awards, free spins and first- and second-screen bonuses—Australian-style games, as the industry calls them. That's only natural, since Aristocrat Leisure, the parent of U.S. subsidiary Aristocrat Technologies, is an Australian firm with more than 50 years in the business. Popular bonusing games include Queen of the Nile and Penguin Pays. Aristocrat also adapts its base games to its Hyperlink progressive system, with four-way progressive jackpots. The jackpot round is played out as a second-screen bonus, as in the railroad-themed Cash Express. The progressive game is played out on the top box coupled with Aristocrat games such as Penguin Pays or Enchanted Forest. During the progressive game, the player pushes buttons to try to stop each spinning reel on a train. On each attempt, the player is awarded points, and the total points for the round determine whether the player wins the Grand, Major, Minor or Mini jackpot. (Most will be Minor or Mini.) A plasma display over an entire bank of machines is active during the progressive round, and when a whole bank is busy, the small progressives hit often enough to grab plenty of attention.

6. H. Bally's is one of the oldest names in gaming, and was the dominant manufacturer of slot machines until IGT took over that role in the 1980s. It made a big push in the late 1990s and the early years of the new millennium to return to prominence by licensing characters, characters and more characters. "We have the best characters in the business," an executive once boasted to me, and there is an incredible list. Betty Boop. Popeye. Dagwood. Blondie. Mr. Magoo. Richie Rich. Assorted *Saturday Night Live* characters, including the Blues Brothers and the Coneheads. Not to mention Bally's licensing agreement with *Playboy*. Bally uses its characters on both reel-spinning and video games, with the reel-spinners including a screen in the top box for bonus rounds on Bally's high-definition EVO Hybrid platform. You can play Popeye as a multi-line, multicoin video slot with bonus rounds on the EVO platform, or play Popeye as a three-reel game, with a bonus round in the top box. The same goes for Ray Charles, Betty Boop and many other Bally characters. Bally has been very creative in progressive slots, making a splash in 2002 with its Cash for Life system in which players can win $1,000 or more per week for the rest of their lives. The company continues to be a force among old-style reel-spinners without bonus rounds, with the classic reel-spinner Blazing 7s. And Bally was the pioneer in multiple-game video machines with the Game Maker, the first machine that allowed the player to touch the screen to choose among a variety of slot and video poker games.

7. J. Atronic, with headquarters in Germany, is one of the world's leading slotmakers, although it is not yet on that level in the United States. It makes video games with extremely sharp graphics and multiple bonus rounds, including both second-screen and first-screen awards. Its Sphinx game has been a major hit, with a bonus round that has players finding their way through obstacles in the Pharaoh's tomb. If they're successful the players move on to another level within the round—Sphinx was one of the first multi-tiered bonus games to reach casino floors. Its success led to Sphinx II, and then Sphinx Gold on the Towerline progressive system that Atronic introduced in 2003. The Towerline games incorporate a high-rising top box with flip cards that spell out "MAGIC BONUS." When the player advances to the bonus round off the video screen, the top-box flip cards stop on potential bonus amounts. Lights surrounding the cards then flash in sequence. When they stop, one remains lit and the player collects the bonus on the corresponding reel. Then the lights flash again, and the player continues collecting bonuses until they stop on a bonus already awarded. When I tested the game Sphinx Gold, a deep voice echoed as if from within the tomb, announcing each bonus award: "FIVE DOLLARS!" "TWENTY-FIVE DOLLARS." There are other, on-screen bonuses too. In Cool Catch, with reel symbols including penguins and ice floes, a fishing bonus has the player touch a penguin on screen to reel in a bonus. Xanadu, all in Asian reds, golds and blacks, uses yin-yang symbols and dragons. It has several bonus rounds, including the Fortune City bonus where players enter the Guards' Chamber to try to find a bonus match among eight stones circling a yin-yang symbol.

8. C. A.C. Coin is as creative as they come in partnering fun bonuses in the top box with reel-spinning games. The company is best known for Slotto, which uses lottery-type balls in a glassed-in top box. The Slotto package is frequently repackaged in fun ways. One that caught my eye at the 2003 Global Gaming Expo was Popcorn. In the Hot Buttered Bonus, the Slotto balls start popping out of a metal tray in a top box designed to look like an old-time movie popcorn machine. Even on video games, the top box remains an entertainment source on A.C. Coin games. On the barbecue-themed King of the Grill, the top box includes a 3-D figure of a pig in chef's hat and apron, carrying a tray of food. When the bonus round launches, the pig descends a column down the center of the box to a barbecue grill, where the embers start to glow. On the screen, the player chooses between two foods to grill. Lighter fluid is splashed on the coals, flames flare up, the food is grilled and reveals whether the player has chosen the larger bonus. The bonus is multi-tiered—the player gets to keep choosing between foods until one is charred to ashes, ending the round.

9. F. Konami, a Japanese company that has been making arcade games since the 1970s, moved into slot manufacturing in the late 1990s. One unique game system has a set of reels inside, facing down. Players can't see the reels themselves, but can see an image reflected off a mirror toward the bottom of the cabinet onto a screen. During regular play, the top half of the screen shows the reels, while the bottom half shows graphics and animation. When the player reaches the bonus round, reels are no longer shown. Instead, the full screen is used for the animated bonus game. I tested a game called Ninja vs. Ninja, one of several using the hybrid format. My bonus round consisted of several levels, trying to find the ninja warrior behind obstacles such as brick walls. Failure to find the warrior ended the round. Konami also makes both video and reel-spinning games, often using the same themes. Mariachi Madness, for example, uses "south of the border" and a bonus in a bullring. On the video game, the bonus is played out on the screen, just like bonuses from other manufacturers. Konami's reel-spinning games have a rectangular color LCD panel in the top box, toward the right side of the reels. That's where the bonus event is played out. Konami's first venture into licensed character games was Rocky, based on the Sylvester Stallone film series—when the game was introduced at the 2002 Global Gaming Expo, Konami set up inside red ropes designed to resemble a boxing ring. One of the most eye-catching products at the 2003 expo was Konami's Fortune Orb, which seats 10 players around an elaborate center display of wheels, ramps and balls that rotate to face a player who reaches the bonus round.

10. G. Mikohn has many fingers in the gaming industry pie. It distributes table games, including Caribbean Stud Poker, designs progressive jackpot systems, and has developed systems for casino accounting and tracking players' wagers. It entered the slot derby in the mid-1990s, and has a reputation for offering video games with bonus rounds in which player skill or knowledge makes a difference. Players answer trivia questions in Trivial Pursuit, narrow suspects in Clue, decide which dice to re-roll in Yahtzee and home in on enemy ships in Battleship. The games don't offer players a mathematical edge, as some video poker games do to experts, but good players will collect larger bonuses than poor ones. Mikohn also makes reel-spinning games with bonus rounds in the top box, such as the pachinko-like Liberty Ball. When the player advances to the bonus round, he or she pushes a button to start a ball dropping among pegs toward bonus-marked slots at the bottom.

KNOW THE MACHINE

1. G. Dilbert's Wheelbert was one of many licensed character-based games introduced by IGT in 2003. It also has a "Wheel of Random Compensation" bonus, with a spinning wheel atop the machine, à la *Wheel of Fortune.*

2. J. The top of Sigma's Big Mouth Billy Bass has a talking fish on a plaque, modeled after the novelty gift that has been heavily advertised on television. On one second-screen bonus, the player has to decide whether to throw back, eat or mount on a plaque a freshly caught fish. Billy, of course, cracks wise throughout.

3. B. *Wheel of Fortune,* in its original reel-spinning version, was IGT's entry into bonus wheel games. It liked the idea so much— along with other games designed by "Wheel of Gold" pioneer Anchor Gaming—that IGT acquired Anchor.

4. E. Based on the popular reality TV show, WMS's *Survivor* puts a high-quality color screen on the top box. Hit the bonus combination on the reels below and it launches the screen up top. You're shown three "challenges": a rope over crocodile-infested waters, a jungle cookout and a fire walk. Push one of three buttons below the screen to choose a challenge. The first time I tested Survivor, I tried the jungle cookout—an animated survivor tossed available edibles and not-so-edibles into a stew pot. A lobster. A snail. Half a coconut. An old sock. The survivor gives each a big "Mmm-mmmm!" and the bonus builds with each new ingredient.

5. I. With the sound and video systems available on today's games, what could be more natural than an Elvis slot machine? After all, the King of Rock 'n' Roll holds the Las Vegas showroom record with 837 consecutive sellouts at the Las Vegas Hilton in the 1970s. IGT introduced the Elvis slot, using Vision Series technology with color LCD panels in the top box, at the 1998 World Gaming Congress. Elvis lives into the early years of the new millennium, and in most jurisdictions is placed as a wide-area progressive game with a huge jackpot.

6. A. Hot Diggity Dog is an attention grabber, as are many A.C. Coin games with top-box bonuses. The game stands tall and is very visible in the casino, and passing customers can't help but stop for a look when the machine's sound system starts playing, "Hot diggity, dog diggity, boom what you do to me."

7. D. Shuffle Master's *Chicago* has several bonus rounds, all harking back to gangland days. In addition to the Tap Dancing bonus, there's another in which the player touches the screen to choose a negative, which develops into a tabloid newspaper front page that screams "MURDER!" or "EXTORTION!" or "KIDNAP-PING!" along with showing a bonus reward.

8. H. With *Men in Black,* based on the hit science-fiction comedy film, WMS plays it to the hilt. The slot cabinet is black. There's a black globe atop the machine, with glowing rings and electric blue lettering that says "MEN IN BLACK" in one hemisphere and "MIB" on the other. The top box includes a starfield on deep black space. And the game itself has multiple bonus rounds with fun animated characters—a must in any WMS game.

9. C. Wink Martindale's Survey of America is typical of Mikohn video products in that a good player can affect the size of the bonus. It's not a true test of knowledge as in Trivial Pursuit or *Ripley's Believe It or Not* trivia questions, but a player who can accurately gauge how an audience of 100 people might have responded will do better than someone taking random guesses.

10. F. Bally Gaming has a series of *Saturday Night Live* games, in both video and reel-spinning formats. The Coneheads video slot has a couple of bonus rounds. One, called the Win Mass Quantities bonus, features a spaceship bouncing off planets on the video screen, with the planets revealing bonus awards. The other is the Senso-Ring Toss, which SNL fans will remember from the old Cone-heads skits in which the adult characters had, ahem, marital relations by tossing rings over each other's cones. On the slot machine, Senso-Ring Toss features animation of either Jane Curtin's Prymaat or Dan Aykroyd's Beldar Conehead character. The player selects a Cone-head, then touches rings on the screen to send them flying toward the cone. The more rings that land on the cone, the bigger the bonus.

Reel Spin No. 6: What Is It?

Slot machines come in several basic types, and the differences are more subtle than just physical reels vs. video reels. Do you know the difference between a multiplier and a buy-a-pay? You should; it makes a difference in whether it's safe to play with less than maximum coins.

See if you can identify these basic types of slot machines:

1. **A multiplier is:**
   A. A reel symbol that multiplies the amount of your winnings.
   B. A slot machine in which winnings are multiplied by the number of coins played.
   C. A coin counter in the change booth or cashier's cage.

2. **A modified multiplier is:**
   A. A reel symbol that multiplies the amount of your winnings even if it lands just above or just below the payline.
   B. A slot machine in which most winnings are multiplied by the number of coins played, but which awards a bonus on the top jackpot with maximum coins played.
   C. A coin counter in the change booth or cashier's cage that has been adapted to count $2 and $5 tokens.

3. A buy-a-pay is:

  A. A slot machine on which each coin played activates a set of reel symbols.

  B. A casino promotion in which players "buy" extra cash with slot club points.

  C. A machine that allows the player a second chance to win by buying an extra spin of one reel.

4. On a progressive slot:

  A. Each winning combination progresses the player toward a bonus jackpot.

  B. Players have a better chance of winning by progressing from one coin played to two coins, to three, then starting the progression over.

  C. A percentage of all coins played are added to the top jackpot.

5. Linked progressives:

  A. Tie together the number of times the player hits specific combinations with the size of the top jackpot.

  B. Double the jackpot when two or more players hit within 24 hours at the same machine.

  C. Electronically link several machines so the jackpot increases on all whenever one or more are played.

6. A "nudge" machine:

  A. Allows players to spin one reel again after a losing spin.

  B. Lets players touch the screen to stop reels in an attempt to force a winning combination.

  C. Moves symbols onto the payline from just above or just under after the reels have stopped spinning.

7. Bonus slots:

  A. Pay bonuses through random hits of a special symbol on the payline.

  B. Allow players to progress to a bonus the longer they play.

  C. Often include a second screen on a video game.

D. Any of the above.

E. None of the above.

8. When slot players refer to a machine as a "doubler," they mean:

A. It has special symbols that double the payout on winning combinations.

B. It allows the player to reinvest winnings, playing a related game on a second screen for double or nothing.

C. It is in a special area of the casino that pays double jackpots on certain days of the week.

9. Second-event games:

A. Are what the casino calls slots farther back in the casino, designed to hold the players' attention after their first gambling event on machines just inside the door.

B. Are slots near the sports book that have LCD panels on which the player can watch sports events.

C. Use regular slot machines as the base game, but give the player an extra way to win.

10. Reel-spinning slots that have bonus rounds:

A. Use a wheel or some other mechanical device in the top box to award a bonus.

B. Sometimes play the base game on reels, but have a video screen in the top box to play the bonus round.

C. Both of the above.

Reel Spin No. 6:
What Is It?
Answers

1. B. A multiplier is a slot machine in which winnings are multiplied by the number of coins played.

An example would be a two-coin machine that with one coin played pays back 1 coin for a single cherry, 2 coins for two cherries, 5 coins for three mixed bars or three cherries, 10 coins for three single bars, 20 coins for three double bars, 40 coins for three triple bars and 100 coins for three 7s.

With two coins played, it simply doubles those payoffs to 2 coins for a single cherry, 4 for two cherries, 10 for three mixed bars or three cherries, 20 for three single bars, 40 for three double bars, 80 for three triple bars and 200 for three 7s.

Nowhere in the pay table is there a bonus for playing the maximum number of coins—or a penalty for playing less than the maximum.

Pure multipliers are not common on regular reel-spinning slots. Usually, there is a bonus at the top of the pay table for playing maximum coins. However, many of the new video slots with multiple paylines and accepting multiple coins per line are multipliers.

2. B. Modified multipliers are the most common slot machines on casino floors. Their pay tables look just like multipliers, except that there is a bonus for playing maximum coins. Usually that bonus is on the top of the pay table.

To carry on with our example from No. 1, let's use a nearly identical two-coin machine. The one-coin pays are the same as in

No. 1, and so are the two-coin pays for everything except three 7s. On three 7s, instead of simply doubling the one-coin payoff of 100 coins to 200 when a second coin is played, the multiplier is modified by kicking the jackpot up to 500 coins. That encourages players to play maximum coins to give themselves a shot at the bonus.

3. A. A buy-a-pay is a slot machine on which each coin activates a set of symbols.

Let's say a machine has symbols of cherries, single bars, double bars, triple bars and 7s. If you play one coin at a time, you're eligible for any cherry payoffs. Play the second coin, and you also get any payoffs on the single bars, double bars and triple bars. The third coin activates the 7s.

That's a buy-a-pay. If you hit three 7s but have played only one coin or two coins, your payoff isn't just reduced—it's reduced to zero. You get no payoff on 7s unless you play the third coin.

Same thing if you've played only one coin and you hit three bars. You get nothing, because you haven't played the second coin to activate the bars.

Multiple-payline machines also are buy-a-pays in that each coin activates a payline. Let's say you're on a three-line, three-coin reel-spinning slot. Play one coin, and you're paid off on any winning combination on the first line. Play two coins, and you get any wins on the first or second line. It takes the third coin before you get any winning combination on any payline. If you play only two coins and three 7s hit on the third line, you're out of luck. It's just another losing spin.

Multiline video slots work in much the same way. On a five-video-reel, five-payline game, you must play at least five coins to activate all the paylines. Be sure to push the "Bet 5 lines" button—it's possible on these games that take multiple coins per line to bet five coins without activating all the lines. You could bet all five coins on one line. The player has to tell the machine what to do.

My wife ran into a similar problem once at the Tropicana in Las Vegas. We sat a few machines apart—I was playing a video poker game, and she was playing a 45-coin video reel slot. The previous player had been playing only four of the five paylines. Marcy planned to play all five, but didn't push the button. And wouldn't you know it. Her first spin came up with five oranges—all on the fifth line. Instead of 300 credits, she got nothing. Ouch.

4. C. On a progressive slot, a percentage of all coins played are added to the top jackpot. Occasionally, you'll run into machines with multiple progressive lines—not only is part of the coins played added to the top jackpot, but a smaller portion is also added to the machine's second biggest payoff, and sometimes even the third biggest.

When the progressive payoff is hit, the player collects the amount of that jackpot, and the progressive meter rolls back to its minimum payoff. For example, the casino paying a progressive jackpot on three 7s might seed the progressive meter at $1,000, then a portion of all bets is added to the jackpot. If it builds to, say, $2,800 before it hits, the winner is paid the $2,800, and the jackpot starts building again from another $1,000.

There is no requirement as to what percentage of coins played must go into the jackpot. A casino with several banks of progressive machines could build the jackpots at different rates, adding half a percent of all coins played here, 1 percent over there and 2 percent on the next floor.

I received a letter from a reader on that very issue. He played a progressive machine for about half an hour, losing $60, and never saw the jackpot meter rise. He complained to a slot manager, who apologized and promised to see if anything was wrong. The player never did get an answer from the casino, and he asked me if there was any requirement on how much of his money had to be added to the meter. There is no such requirement.

5. C. Linked progressive systems link several machines so that the jackpot on all increases whenever one machine is played.

When you see a big, lighted sign that practically screams "$5,847.23!" or "$27,529.11" or even "$26,912,183.29," you've found the linked progressives. The games don't have to be exactly the same—a bank of progressives might link Double Diamonds, Triple Diamonds, Wild Cherry, Red White and Blue, and Five Times Pay machines all to the same jackpot meter. Sometimes the casino operator will theme the progressive area, maybe using all Double Diamonds machines to make a Diamonds Jackpot alcove.

Progressives with enormous, lifestyle-changing jackpots in the hundreds of thousands or even tens of millions of dollars usually link several casinos in what are called "wide-area progressives." There are exceptions. Caesars Palace's Million Dollar Baby slots are exclusive to Caesars. But one casino could never support the kind of jackpot available in Nevada on IGT's Megabucks machines, with jackpots that have surpassed $39 million. That's a lot of customers dropping in their three bucks per pull to nudge the progressive meter up pennies at a time. Make a maximum-coins bet in a Megabucks machine at the Barbary Coast in Las Vegas, and the progressive meters also rise at McCarran Airport, Harrah's in Lake Tahoe and every other Nevada casino with Megabucks machines.

For many years, all the dominant multi-casino progressives were IGT games—Megabucks, Quartermania and Nevada Nickels adapt regular IGT reel-spinners such as Red White and Blue or Double Diamonds to the progressive system. On a Double Diamonds machine adapted for Megabucks, Double Diamonds symbols on the payline on all reels still bring a jackpot, but not *the* jackpot. That's reserved for lining up all Megabucks symbols.

In the late 1990s and the early years of the new millennium, other manufacturers bid for a piece of the action with wide-area progressives. Bally Gaming introduced its Thrillions system, which allows nickel, quarter and dollar players all to go for the same linked jackpot. The math of the game works out so that quarter players are more likely to strike it rich than nickel players, and dollar players have a better chance than quarter players. There are several different Bally games on the link, the best known probably being Betty Boop, but with character-driven games such as *Blondie* and Popeye also on the link.

WMS Gaming, a company on the rise through the late 1990s with its innovative use of video and animation, used its popular Monopoly series to launch its entry into the wide-area market. At the 2003 Global Gaming Expo, the gaming industry's fall trade show, where manufacturers introduce their latest and greatest to potential buyers, WMS showed off Monopoly Money, which, in addition to offering a progressive jackpot, uses animation of Mr. Monopoly within a giant, color-changing Monopoly Money display in the top box to guide the player through a bonus round. At the same show, Atronic touted its Towerline wide-area progressives. The system, which had been launched in the previous year in Arizona as "Arizona Magic," uses several Atronic base games, along with flip cards that spell out "MAGIC BONUS" in the top box. When the player advances to the bonus round, the cards flip to reveal potential bonus amounts.

There are some big differences between single-casino progressives and the multi-casino systems. On most single-casino systems, the casino owns the machines outright and collects all the profit they generate. Wide-area progressives are "revenue participation games." Revenue is shared by the manufacturer and the operator.

One point to remember on all progressives is that the machine has to generate enough revenue between jackpots to pay for the eventual big hit and still leave a profit. Most times that you play you won't hit the big one, and you'll find that the small payoffs come less frequently than on regular slot machines. I usually don't play big-money progressives, although at the end of a Las Vegas trip during which other games had been particularly good to me, I couldn't resist investing $100 to stalk that Megabucks monster. That the monster got me instead was no great surprise.

6. C. A nudge machine moves symbols onto the payline from just above or just below. The most common nudge machine is a version of Double Diamonds in which some of the bars, double bars and single bars cross diamond symbols with the points facing down, and others cross diamonds with the points facing up. If a point-down diamond lands just above, it drops down to the payline. If a point-up diamond lands just below, it clicks up to the payline.

That makes it possible for the player to have a winning spin even if no symbols land on the payline when the reels first stop. In fact, it's inevitable—anyone who plays this machine for very long will have that happen. I even had it happen on a Double Diamonds machine adapted to Megabucks, chasing that $26 million jackpot in November 1998. Just above the payline I had double bars with down-points on the first and third reels. Just below the payline, I had a triple bar with a up-point on the second reel. Nudge, nudge, nudge—and I had a 15-coin payoff.

As king of the reel-spinners, IGT is also king of the nudge machines. On Balloon Bars, hot air balloons rise to the payline when they land just below. On Jurassic Slots, if the dinosaur's head points down, the symbol drops to the payline; if the dinosaur's head points up, he rises. It's the same basic idea as the Double Diamonds nudge machines. Only the artwork is different.

7. D. Bonus slots can pay off through a random hit of a special symbol on the payline, as in *Wheel of Fortune* when the "Spin the Wheel" symbol on the payline enables the player to push a button for a wheel spin that reveals the bonus payoff.

One of the earliest slots that allowed players to progress to a bonus the longer they play was Odyssey's Fort Knox. There, each spin of the reels was accompanied by an on-screen meter running through random digits. If the digit matched its counterpart in a 10-digit series, the player advanced one step to cracking the code to unlock the vault at Fort Knox and get his bonus payoff.

The kings of the bonus rounds are the second-screen events. Let's use WMS Gaming's Jackpot Party as an example. Games and themes come and go, but Jackpot Party is one that has stood the test of time in several formats. It started life as a three-reel, five-payline reel-spinning slot with a Dotmation screen in the top box to play a bonus round. In the late '90s, it was adapted as a video game, and has proved remarkably durable. It was reworked as a three-reel video slot with a simplified bonus round in 2002, then became one of the first games released on WMS's new high-definition CPU-NXT video game systems in 2003.

In the five-reel video and five-payline reel versions, Jackpot Party's bonus round is triggered when the player lands three party noisemakers on the paylines—they don't have to line up. On the machine's audio, a crowd cheers "Jackpot Party!" and disco music plays. On reel slots, the Dotmation screen shows rows of dotted squares, and on video games, the screen shows rows of gift-wrapped packages. Under each is either a bonus amount, or "Pooper"—a cop or a disgruntled neighbor. The player collects bonuses by touching packages on the video screen or pushing a button on the slot console to select Dotmation squares. Rewards mount until the player chooses a Pooper, ending the round.

Jackpot Party, durable and entertaining as it is, was part of the first generation of bonus slots with a single bonus round. Today, many games include multiple bonus events. On WMS's Cash Crop, for instance, one bonus round has an animated farmer growing crops and the player choosing plants for bonuses. If the player suc-cessfully chooses three plants from one crop, the farmer plants another, higher-paying crop. The player continues, and bonuses mount, until a gopher pops up from beneath the chosen plant, ending the round. A second bonus round sends the player to a county fair to choose the animated contestant whose veggies will take the prize. The player gets a bonus no matter what, but it's biggest if his or her chosen contestant takes the blue ribbon.

Sometimes there are bonus rounds within bonus rounds. In Atronic's Mystery Mask, introduced at the 2003 Global Gaming Expo, the dominant symbol on the machine glass is a haunting Phantom of the Opera–style mask resting upon a piano keyboard. There's a two-level bonus round in which the player first chooses among candles on a screen to reveal bonus amounts. Sometimes a candle will hide a mystery symbol that unlocks catacombs in which the player tries to find the game's Disguised Man or Dis-guised Lady for a bigger bonus.

8. A. A doubler is a slot machine that has special symbols that double the payoffs when used in winning combinations.

The grandaddy of doublers is IGT's Double Jackpot. It's a 1980s-era machine that's no longer one of the most popular games around, but it still has a place on many casino floors. The concept is simple. Let's say three triple bars are worth 80 coins. Hit two triple bars and a Double Jackpot symbol, and the payoff is doubled to 160 coins. Hit one triple bar and two Double Jackpot symbols, and the payoff is doubled again to 320 coins. Hit three Double Jackpot symbols, and you hit the jackpot.

IGT has refined that concept and used it over and over. Double Diamonds, Triple Diamonds, Five Times Pay and Ten Times Pay all work on the same basic principle. A winning combination with one Five Times Pay combination is quintupled; with two Five Times Pay symbols, the payoff is multiplied by 25.

Other manufacturers have tried to get in on the action. Sigma, with its Treasure Tunnel games, multiplies payoffs by two, three, four or five times when the Treasure Tunnel symbol is part of a winning combination. Williams uses its dotmation screen to multiply payoffs up to 125 times on MegaMultiplier 125.

But Double Diamonds and Five Times Pay are tried and true, drawing consistent play even while flashier games carve out their niches.

9. C. Second-event games use regular slot machines as a base game, but offer an extra way to win. Wheel of Gold, the forerunner of *Wheel of Fortune* and other wheel-spinning slots, was the first big hit game to offer a second event. The basic games were slant-top versions of old reliables like Wild Cherry, Red White and Blue, and Double Diamonds. Reels were adapted to include a "Spin the Wheel" symbol, which would yield a spin of the bonus wheel atop a column affixed to the back of the machine.

The first time I saw Wheel of Gold, I was amazed by customers' reactions. Every time a tone sounded to alert players that someone had hit a Spin the Wheel symbol, heads spun as quickly as the wheel. Everyone at the bank of machines stopped to watch the wheel, and so did passers-by. It was an attention grabber, pure and simple.

10. C. Reel-spinning slots that have bonus rounds sometimes use a wheel or some other mechanical device in the top box to award a bonus, and sometimes play the base game on reels, but have a video screen in the top box to play the bonus round.

We've talked about Wheel of Gold and *Wheel of Fortune,* with the spinning wheel in the top box. There are many other top-box bonus devices on reel-spinners. A.C. Coin has a hit with its Slotto series, which uses lottery-style balls in its top box for bonus awards. The company has found some fun, creative ways to use Slotto. In Popcorn, a machine designed to look like an old-time popcorn wagon, when the popcorn symbol lands on the payline of the reel-spinning game, the Slotto balls start popping out of a metal pan at the top to award a bonus—three Slotto balls if the player has won a large bag of popcorn, two for medium or one for small.

IGT uses a lighted column of cash and a video screen in the top box for Regis' Cash Club, with video of Regis Philbin and weighty chords not unlike the sounds of *Who Wants to Be a Millionaire.* The game has five spinning reels, and has two bonus rounds—one in which Regis prompts the player to push buttons to move the lights up a column to higher bonus amounts, and a "check writing bonus" in which Regis writes a "check" on the video screen, then says, "You wanted something bigger, didn't you?" He'll rewrite, then maybe even rewrite again before giving the final bonus.

WMS's game based on the reality TV series *Survivor* is a reel-spinner with a video screen in the top box for a pick-the-survivor bonus round. Bally Gaming also makes extensive use of top-box video with reel spinning games in its EVO-Hybrid game platform, with licensed games such as *To Tell the Truth* and *Playboy.*

Reel Spin No. 7: How They Work

When a player sits down to play blackjack, he can get an intuitive feel for his chances of winning—he can see how the cards add up to potential winning combinations. Same at the craps table; it's not difficult to fathom how a roll of two dice determines winners and losers. But at a slot machine all the action leading to winning spins and losing spins is out of the player's view.

See how much you know about how slot machines, and the odds of winning, work:

1. **The device with inner workings most like a modern slot machine is:**
   A. A 1960s slot machine.
   B. A coin-operated gumball machine.
   C. An electric clock.
   D. A personal computer.

2. **The odds of winning on an old-style mechanical slot machine are determined by:**
   A. The number of symbols and spaces on each reel.
   B. The number of reels.
   C. Both of the above.
   D. None of the above.

3. **The odds of winning on a modern electronic slot machine are determined by:**
   A. The number of symbols and spaces on each reel.
   B. The number of reels.
   C. Both of the above.
   D. None of the above.

4. **As compared with a mechanical slot machine, a computerized machine has:**
   A. A higher hit frequency.
   B. A lower hit frequency.
   C. About the same hit frequency.
   D. There's no way to tell.

5. **Compared with a three-reel reel-spinning slot, a five-reel video slot machine usually has:**
   A. A higher hit frequency.
   B. A lower hit frequency.
   C. About the same hit frequency.
   D. There's no way to tell.

6. **A machine is programmed to pay a jackpot about once per 10,000 pulls. You have played 9,999 pulls without hitting a jackpot. The odds of hitting on the next pull are:**
   A. Even.
   B. 1 in 100.
   C. 1 in 10,000.
   D. Undetermined.

7. **A machine is programmed to pay a jackpot about once per 10,000 pulls. You just won a jackpot on your last pull. The odds of hitting again on the next pull are:**
   A. 1 in 10,000.
   B. 1 in 100,000.
   C. 1 in 1 million.
   D. Undetermined.

8. **After playing a slot machine for two hours, you walk away. The player who replaces you immediately hits the jackpot. If you had stayed:**

   A. You'd have hit the jackpot.

   B. You'd have had about a 50 percent chance of hitting the jackpot.

   C. You'd have had about a 25 percent chance of hitting the jackpot.

   D. Your chances of hitting the jackpot would have been very small.

9. **After losing for most of a session, you walk away. The player who replaces you quickly has several hits in a row. If you had stayed:**

   A. You'd have had equal success.

   B. The details might have been different, but the machine would have warmed up for you.

   C. The machine would have stayed cold.

   D. There's no way to determine what you'd have hit.

10. **If a machine has a video screen instead of physical reels the odds of winning:**

    A. Increase.

    B. Decrease.

    C. Are about the same.

    D. Could be any of the above.

11. **Among the most common slot machines, the best payback percentages are usually found on:**

    A. Dollar machines.

    B. Half-dollar machines.

    C. Quarter machines.

    D. Nickel machines.

12. On the average, playing an equal number of coins, the player will lose the most money on:
   A. Dollar machines.
   B. Half-dollar machines.
   C. Quarter machines.
   D. Nickel machines.

13. On reel-spinning machines, the payback percentage is usually highest:
   A. If the player plays one coin at a time.
   B. If the player plays maximum coins.
   C. If the player mixes a pattern of maximum, minimum and in-between bets.
   D. The number of coins played makes no difference.

14. A player who wagers one coin at a time should play:
   A. Progressives.
   B. Buy-a-pays.
   C. Multipliers.
   D. None of the above.

15. A player who wagers one coin at a time should *never* play:
   A. Progressives.
   B. Buy-a-pays.
   C. Multipliers.
   D. Any slot machine.

16. A player who usually bets three quarters at a time might find a higher payback percentage with similar risk by playing:
   A. One coin at a time in dollar machines.
   B. Three nickels per payline in five-line, multiple-coin video slots.
   C. Both of the above.
   D. None of the above.

17. Slot players increase their chances of winning by playing:
   A. Slots on which they have seen other players winning.

   B. Slots on which they have seen other players losing.

   C. Slots that haven't been played in a few hours.

   D. None of the above.

18. The highest-paying slots in the United States are in:

   A. Nevada.

   B. Mississippi.

   C. Colorado.

   D. Missouri.

19. In Las Vegas, the highest paying slots are:

   A. On the Strip.

   B. Downtown.

   C. In north Las Vegas.

   D. At the airport.

20. Two identical-looking slot machines sit side by side, with the same pay tables. From that, we know:

   A. They have the same long-run payback percentage.

   B. They have the same long-run hit frequency on small payoffs.

   C. They will pay the top jackpot about as often as one another.

   D. None of the above.

Reel Spin No. 7: How They Work Answers

1. D. Modern slot machines are most like personal computers. In fact, they *are* computers, continuously running a slot machine program. Machines are driven by microprocessors, with programs on chips—different chips for different portions of the game. One chip holds the random number generator (RNG) that determines the combinations you see on the reels or screen. It is a separate program from the accounting programs and slot club program—the RNG doesn't know how many coins you've bet or whether you're using a club card. It just generates the numbers that correspond to reel combinations, and can't give you fewer hits because you've bet more money or because you're using a club card.

2. C. On mechanical slot machines, the number of symbols and spaces on each reel together with the number of reels determine the odds.

To use a simple example, let's take a three-reel mechanical with 10 symbols on each reel, and no spaces landing on the payline. This is a real situation, by the way. Some early slot machines were configured in this way.

One of the symbols on each reel is for the top jackpot. The jackpot symbol has 1 chance in 10 of landing on the payline on any given reel. The chances of all three jackpot symbols landing on the payline are 1 in 10x10x10, or in 1 in 1,000. The player could expect to hit the jackpot about once in 1,000 pulls.

With those kinds of odds, what kind of jackpot do you think a slot machine could offer? It certainly couldn't offer the multimillion-dollar jackpots today's slots offer. It couldn't offer even a 1,000-coin jackpot—if it did, all pulls other than the top jackpot would have to be losers for the machine to break even. Would the proprietor allow players to plunk in 1,000 coins, one coin at a time, and hit a 1,000-coin jackpot? Nope. No profit for the machine. And the players would get bored, too. No small payouts to keep them interested.

So, given that the operator is going to have to keep something as profit and that some pulls would have to yield smaller payoffs to players, how much do you think could be paid as the top jackpot? One hundred coins? A 100-coin jackpot was huge. Twenty coins is more like it.

How to offer a bigger jackpot? The first step is to put more stops on the reels. With 10 symbols and 10 spaces, or 20 stops, the odds against hitting the top jackpot grow to 7,999:1, or 1 chance in 8,000. Increase the size of the reel and make it 30 stops, and the jackpot chances become 1 in 27,000.

Another solution is to add a fourth reel. With 30 stops, including one jackpot symbol per reel, there is 1 chance in 810,000 of hitting the big one. Now jackpots in the tens of thousands of coins can be awarded.

That's still not the kind of prizes today's players seek. That would have to wait for more sophisticated systems.

3. D. Neither the number of stops per reel nor the number of reels on a machine determine the odds on computerized slots.

In fact, the reels are just a representation of what's happening in the random number generator (RNG). The RNG continuously generates numbers that correspond to reel stops. The reel-stop numbers generated as the customer initiates play determine the outcome of that pull. The machine then spins the reels to give the player a visual representation of that random number.

No matter how many reels and how many symbols there are, the odds on a computerized slot machine can be virtually anything the manufacturer programs them to be.

It is possible on a computerized slot to have a three-reel machine that awards jackpots in the millions of dollars.

Are results random on computerized slots? Yes, but it's the RNG's output that is subject to state randomness standards. Not every symbol has an equal chance of landing on the payline, as on a mechanical machine. To oversimplify a bit, the RNG could be programmed with 1 million numbers, with only one number corresponding to three 7s and 20,000 numbers corresponding to three single bars. Each single bar on the physical reel would land on the payline much more often than each 7. But randomness standards would be satisfied as long as the three 7s number has an equal chance of being selected as *any one* of the 20,000 numbers corresponding to three bars.

When I first started writing about casino games in 1994, I had a conversation about slots with the late video poker guru Lenny Frome. Lenny had been an engineer in the aerospace industry, and in his retirement he took on casino games. He not only devised winning strategies for video poker players, but also did the math for games developers looking to take new games to state gaming boards for licensing.

"The average player doesn't understand," he told me, "that you can take a slot machine with three reels and 10 stops per reel, have a 7 on every stop on the first two reels and nine stops on the third reel. Put one blank space on the third reel. Now there are 1,000 possible combinations, and 900 of them are three 7s, right? You can program that machine so that the blank space will come up 999 times out of 1,000. Or 9,999 times out of 10,000. Or even 999,999 out of 1 million."

In case of a dispute, those random numbers, and not the visual representation on the reels, are considered the actual outcome. The glass on slot machines usually carries a message that says, "Malfunction voids play," or something to that effect. If the combination on the reels does not match the machine's electronic record of what the RNG says should have been the combination, that is regarded as a malfunction. In such cases, the casino can deny a jackpot, and jackpots have been voided by such malfunctions.

Some states require the casino to deny a jackpot if the reel combination doesn't match the electronic record. That is in part an anti-cheating regulation. A player who has learned to manipulate the reel combination on a machine is unlikely also to be able to manipulate the machine's electronic record.

4. D. A computerized slot could have a higher hit frequency than a mechanical version, or a lower hit frequency, or the same. It depends on the programming.

The hit frequency, by the way, refers to the percentage of all spins that give the player some kind of winning combination. The majority will be low-paying hits—a cherry here, three mixed bars there. Some video slots—some in IGT's video *Wheel of Fortune* series, for example—have hit frequencies in excess of 50 percent. The player will get something back on more than half the spins. However, most of those hits return fewer coins than are wagered.

Slot directors have a continuing dilemma over whether they should offer machines with relatively high hit frequencies and low jackpots, or high jackpots and low hit frequencies. Does the big jackpot attract the players, or will having a steadier stream of small hits better keep them in their seats?

Two machines with the same payback percentage can have wildly different personalities. A machine with a large jackpot has to make its profit by giving the player fewer and smaller paybacks between big hits. A reel-spinning machine that frequently gives the player something back, even if it's just six coins for a cherry or 10 coins for three mixed bars, doesn't bank enough during normal play to pay out a big jackpot.

Some players like chasing the big hit; others like the machine giving them back enough in smaller payouts to keep them going a while. Most would like both in the same machine, but fiscal reality makes that rare. Slot directors try to keep a variety of both types on the floor—machines with big jackpots and machines with high hit frequencies—as well as machines that fall somewhere in the middle on both scales.

5. A. Compared with a three-reel reel-spinning slot, a five-reel video slot machine usually has a higher hit frequency.

Most three-reel slots have a single payline, although some have three and a handful even have five. Five-reel video slots all have multiple paylines, with five being the fewest on the market. The most common number is nine, and it's not unusual to find video slots with 10, 15 or 20 paylines. If the player bets at least one coin on each payline on a nine-line game, that's at least a nine-coin wager. With that bet size, it's relatively easy to devise a game that will give a player frequent hits of fewer coins than were bet. Maybe the player has lost one coin on each of eight paylines, but has won five for the one coin wagered on the other line. The game can return two or five or seven coins on a spin, and the player still feels like he or she has done something. The player gets a little boost from "winning," but at the same time the machine is keeping a little something to offset other, bigger wins.

Not so on three-reel slots. If there's only one payline, and the player making minimum bets is wagering only one coin at a time, there is no way to give the player a "win" of less than the wager. On some three-reelers, if the player makes a maximum bet of three coins, three blank spaces will return two coins to the player, but even then the machine socks away only one coin on the spin.

The result is that video games are programmed with much higher hit frequencies than reel-spinning games. Most video slots give the player something back, even if it's less than the wager, on 40 percent or so of spins. Some exceed a 50 percent hit frequency. On reel-spinners, hit frequencies tend to be 15 percent or less. Bally Gaming's Betty Boop Blazing 7s, regarded as a high-hit-frequency game for reel machines, is made available to operators with hit frequencies ranging from 12.7 to 13.6 percent.

Does that mean that payback percentages are higher on video than on reel games? No. Winning spins on reel-spinning games usually pay several times the bet size, while the majority of "wins" on video games are smaller than the bet. That makes up the difference in the hit frequencies, but it also makes reel slots more volatile than video slots. Reel slots will yield both more big wins and more fast losses. Video slots tend to be more of an even-keel game, keeping the player at the machine longer than a reel slot on a losing streak, but in the end they'll keep just as high a percentage of your money.

6. C. If a machine programmed to pay the top jackpot an average of once per 10,000 pulls has gone 9,999 pulls without a jackpot, the odds are still 1 in 10,000.

Let's start with a little disclaimer. I am not saying that slot machines pay the top jackpot once per 10,000 pulls. Some pay much more frequently—I once came across specifications for a $5 slot with a relatively small top jackpot that came up with the big hit better than once per 1,000 pulls. On the other hand, John Robison, author of *The Slot Expert's Guide to Playing Slots,* found a PC sheet for Megabucks that put the odds of hitting the top jackpot at 1 in 50 million. Different machines serve different purposes, and will have different jackpot odds.

Now, then, we're assuming a game with a 1 in 10,000 chance of hitting the jackpot. Each spin of the reels is an independent event. The last pull, or the last 10,000 pulls, have no bearing on what the next one will bring.

In the long run, the random number generator in our example will generate the jackpot enough times that the average will come out to about once per 10,000 pulls. However, a cold streak with no jackpots does not have to even out precisely in any number of pulls. Going 10,000 pulls without a jackpot does not mean the next 10,000 pulls should include two jackpots. In fact, the best guess is that the next 10,000 pulls will include one jackpot, just the same as the expectation for any other 10,000 pulls.

Eventually, the cold streak fades into statistical insignificance. The most likely result for 1 million pulls is 100 jackpots. If you've gone 10,000 pulls without one, the most likely result for the next 990,000 pulls is 99 jackpots—one jackpot per 10,000 pulls. If that were to occur, it would mean the machine had paid 99 jackpots in 1 million pulls, or an average of one per 10,101. That's close enough to the 1 in 10,000 expected average that we can say the machine is right on it.

There is no need for the machine ever to play catch-up, and it doesn't. Past results have no bearing on future spins.

7. A. If you have just hit a jackpot on a machine programmed to pay an average of one jackpot per 10,000 pulls, your odds of hitting again on the next pull are the same as when you started—1 in 10,000.

Most players think the odds are closer to 1 in 1 million, and few will play a machine that they know has just paid out a big jackpot. They have a misconception of how the machine works, and they also have a misconception of how odds work.

As we discussed in No. 6, every spin is an independent trial, and past results have no bearing on future outcomes. If the random number generator is programmed to spit out the jackpot combination once per 10,000 pulls, then there is 1 chance in 10,000 on every pull, regardless of what happened on the last spin.

That leads us to the misconception on how the odds work. If, before you pull the handle on this machine with one jackpot per 10,000 pulls, you ask me the odds of hitting the big one on the next two spins, I will tell you 1 in 100 million. The odds of hitting the first one are 1 in 10,000, the odds of hitting the second are 1 in 10,000, and to get the odds of hitting twice in a row we multiply those chances by each other, and get 1 in 100 million.

However, after you've hit the jackpot for the first time, the odds of hitting the second in a row revert to 1 in 10,000. We're no longer linking two future events. You've already hit one jackpot; it's no longer a factor in the equation. Now we're just weighing your chances of hitting on one pull, and that's the same 1 in 10,000 as on any other pull.

If you should hit twice in a row, the machine doesn't have to go ice cold to make up for it. Over the next 10,000 spins, the best guess is that it will pay out one jackpot. Over the next 999,998 spins—which added to our two, give us a cool million—the best guess is that we'll hit the same 100 jackpots as would be the average for any other million spins. If we do just that, and have 102 jackpots instead of 100 in 1 million spins, that makes the average

1 per 9,804 spins—close enough to 1 in 10,000 that we're just about there with no abnormal cold streaks. Our hot streak doesn't need to be balanced off by a cold wave. In the long run, it just fades into statistical insignificance.

8. D. If you walk away from a machine and the player who replaces you immediately hits the jackpot, it's highly unlikely that you would have hit the same jackpot. Your timing would have had to be the same down to the same exact microsecond. If you were the tiniest fraction of a second slower or faster on the trigger, or if you would have stopped to do anything else but hit the button, or if your replacement did anything but mimic your exact timing and rhythm, the random number generator would have been at a different point and your results would have been different. The chances that you'd have hit that jackpot are very, very small.

9. D. We can know nothing of what you would have done had you stayed at the machine, except that your results would have been different from the player who replaced you. In longer streaks, differences in timing are multiplied. The odds against you having the same streak are astronomical.

The basic message here is this: Don't worry about how other players fare on a machine you've vacated. Your results would have been different anyway. If success by another player on "your" machine is going to bother you, walk to another part of the casino and don't look back.

10. D. Odds on a video reel slot could be better than odds on a machine with moving reels. They could also be worse, or about the same. Video slots are programmed in much the same way—there is a random number generator that continuously generates numbers corresponding to reel combinations until it receives a signal that you're going to play. Odds can be programmed in the same way as on reel slots.

You could have five video slots and five reel-spinners standing in a row, and it's possible the five video slots could all have higher payback percentages than the five reel-spinners. It's also possible the five reel-spinners could all have higher payback percentages than the five video slots. More likely is that some of each would be near the top, and some of each would be near the bottom.

There is no way to tell by looking at them. Only the manufacturers and slot managers who know what chips are in what machines know for sure.

11. A. Usually, the higher denomination of coin played in a slot machine, the higher the payback percentage.

We can see that in some of the statistics from various state gaming boards. On the Las Vegas Strip, nickel slots return about 90 percent, quarters about 93 percent, half-dollars about 94 percent and dollars a little better than 95 percent. In Atlantic City, there are few nickels, but percentages rise from about 90 percent on quarters, 91 on half dollars and 92 on dollars.

In nearly every gaming jurisdiction, five-dollar machines will pay a higher denomination than dollar games, which will pay more than quarters, which will pay more than nickels, which will pay more than pennies.

12. A. Even though dollar slots usually offer a higher payback percentage than lower denominations, players lose more money in the more expensive machines.

Let's look at it this way. We're playing in a casino that averages 95 percent payback on dollar slots and 93 percent on quarters. You start with 100 credits on a dollar slot machine. I move over to a quarter machine and start with 100 credits there. We each run our money through the machine once.

On the average, you finish with 95 credits and I finish with 93. Your payback percentage is higher than mine. But the five credits you've lost are worth $5, and the seven I've lost are worth $1.75. You've done better than I have on a percentage basis, but you've also lost more money.

In real life, things won't work out so neatly. A 95 percent pay-back percentage doesn't mean you always wind up with 95 coins for every 100 you wager. If it did, we wouldn't play the slots—we could just hand the casino manager a $5 bill and say, "Here, I was going to run $100 through that slot machine. You just keep this."

No, we hold out hope that sometimes we're going to win. And we will. Not only that, the higher the payback percentage, the better our shot that we'll have a winning session. If you start with $100 on a dollar slot and I start with $25—100 coins—on a quarter machine, you'll win more often than I will. But remember that your risk is higher, too, and balance that against your bankroll.

13. B. While the situation is somewhat different on video slots, the payback percentage on reel-spinners is usually highest if the player bets maximum coins.

That's because on most reel-spinning machines there is a reward for making the maximum bet. On progressive machines, we're not eligible for the jackpot unless we bet the maximum. On buy-a-pays, we either don't get paid on all potential winning combinations or we don't get paid on all paylines without that max bet.

On the most common slots, with modified multiplier pay tables, the reward in playing maximum coins is a jump in the top jackpot. How much of a difference does that make? Let's set up an example.

We've received information that a particular slot machine is programmed to pay 95 percent in the long run with the maximum three coins bet. Not only that, we know that three 7s land on the payline an average of once per 10,000 pulls. (This wouldn't happen in real life; we can't tell payback percentages by looking at a machine and the casino won't tell us.) We see that most paybacks are proportional—for example, three mixed bars pay us 5 coins for one played, 10 for two and 15 for three.

The exception is at the top of the pay table. If we're lucky enough to hit three 7s, we get 1,000 coins if we've played one coin and 2,000 if we've played two, but our payback jumps to 4,500 coins if we've bet the max.

If we bet the max for 10,000 spins, we would wager 30,000 coins, and if we got the 95 percent payback our return would be 28,500 coins. Of that return, 4,500 would be the payoff the one time we hit three 7s. That leaves 24,000 coins returned to us for smaller hits.

Those smaller paybacks are proportional, so we've received 8,000 coins in small hits for our first coin wagered, 8,000 for our second coin and 8,000 for our third. We'll add the jackpot payoff separately—three 7s with one coin played would have given us 1,000 coins, so we add that to the 8,000 in small hits and get a total 9,000-coin return on our 10,000 first coins. Our payback percentage on our first coin is 90 percent.

It works the same way on our second coin—an 8,000-coin return on small hits, 1,000 coins on three 7s for a total 9,000-coin payback, or 90 percent.

If we played one coin at a time in this machine, that's just what we would get: a 90 percent payback, even though the machine is certified at 95 percent.

The difference is the jackpot bonus on the third coin. Just as on the first two, the third coin brings us an 8,000-coin payback on small hits on the third. But the jackpot on three 7s jumps from 2,000 coins for two coins played to 4,500 for the third. The difference—2,500 coins—is what we add to the small returns to give us our total payback on the third coins. And we see that the 10,000 coins we've invested as the third coins of our wager bring us a total return of 10,500 coins.

Our return on the third coin is 105 percent. We've paid our dues with the first two coins, and gotten a little back on the third one.

Whether the third coin is actually profitable on a real machine is iffy. It depends on the size of the final-coin jackpot jump as well as how often that jackpot hits. Some machines do actually pay more than 100 percent on the final coin; some do not.

But on all slot machines that boost the jackpot for maximum-coin play, the payback percentage is higher than the machine's overall average if maximum coins are played, and lower than the machine's average if fewer coins are wagered.

On video slots, few machines have such incentives designed into the game. It's best to play all the paylines—you wouldn't want to lose a chance at a second-screen bonus because the bonus symbols landed on a line you weren't playing—but there is no disproportionate increase on the pay table for betting maximum coins, and the payback percentage will be the same regardless of whether you bet one coin per line or 20.

The biggest exception appears to be on video slots with a progressive jackpot, such as Aristocrat's Hyperlink four-way progressive system with bonus rounds such as the railroad-themed Cash Express. In those games you're not eligible for the top progressive if you don't bet the max. Just as on reel-spinners, if you don't want to bet the max, play non-progressive machines.

14. C. Players who bet one coin at a time should seek out reel-spinning multipliers, with pay tables that increase proportionally with each coin bet. If you stick to pure multipliers, your long-term payback percentage will be the same regardless of how many coins you play.

If you can't find a pure multiplier, play a multiplier with the top of the pay table modified to give a bonus for maximum coins played. You'll get a lower percentage than if you'd played maximum coins, but most of the pay table is proportional and you won't be penalized as badly as if you'd played certain other machines.

15. A and B. Never play a progressive machine with less than maximum coins.

Likewise, never play a buy-a-pay with less than maximum coins. I once was playing at Empress Casino in Joliet, Illinois, and players in the row to my back started shrieking, "Look at you! Congratulations! What's that worth?"

I turned around. A woman behind me and a couple of machines to my left had three jackpot symbols on the payline. After a minute or two, with no coins clanking into the tray, no credits mounting on the meter and no lights flashing to signal an attendant, the woman's face clouded.

"This machine must be broken," she deduced. "Why am I not getting anything?"

She wasn't getting anything because she was at a buy-a-pay, and she had played only one coin. The jackpot symbols were activated only by the third coin played. With one or two coins, jackpot symbols were just more losers.

"I didn't know that. Why don't they tell you that?"

They do. It's on the machine glass. Read the glass before you play and understand just what it takes to win. If you find yourself at a machine that divides the pay table into first-coin winners, second-coin winners and third-coin winners, and you want to play one or two coins at a time, move to a different machine.

16. A. A player who usually risks three coins at a time might find a higher payback percentage playing one coin at a time in dollar slots.

The average payback percentage on dollar slots is higher than on quarter slots. If you find a dollar multiplier, with no bonus for maximum coins played, there's a good chance your payback for one coin will be higher than if you play three coins in a quarter slot. But if the top of the dollar pay table is modified to reward maximum-coins players, the payback for playing one coin at a time will be lower than the machine's overall average.

Nickel video slots are another matter. In the first edition of this book, I noted that most video slots are true multipliers, and that betting less than the max doesn't decrease your payback percentage. The early information I had at the time was that slot directors recognized that nickel players on multicoin machines were actually averaging a higher wager per spin than quarter three-reel players, and that payback percentages on the nickel games would reflect that.

Unfortunately, that is not the way things unfolded. Paybacks on nickel video slots are much lower than those on quarter reel-spinners in virtually every jurisdiction—in 2003, quarters were outpaying nickels by about 93 percent to 91 percent in Mississippi, 92.5 to 88 in Illinois, 91 to 89 in New Jersey and 93 to 90 on the Las Vegas Strip. A player betting the same amount on a nickel machine as on a quarter machine is getting a lower payback percentage, not a higher or even equal one.

17. D. In makes no difference if other players have been winning or losing on a particular machine, or if the machine hasn't been played in a while. Past results have no bearing on future play.

To be terribly unscientific about this, here are two incidents that happened two days apart on a trip to Las Vegas.

I was playing at the Flamingo Hilton, and sat down at an empty Red White and Blue machine. A couple of machines down the row, a gentleman looked at me, grabbed his arms and said, "Brrrrrrrr!"

"Chilly?" I asked.

"Frigid," he replied. "I played that machine earlier this morning. Nothin'. I saw a guy and his girlfriend play it later, and they didn't hit anything, either."

Being exceptionally hard-headed, I slid my $20 bill in anyway. My third pull was three blue 7s. A few minutes later I hit three triple bars. Then three mixed 7s—a white and two blues. I walked away with more than $200.

A couple of days later, I was walking down a row of slots at Circus Circus. A man and a woman hit three mixed 7s.

"I don't believe it," the woman cried.

"Another one!" the man enthused.

They drew me aside. "This is incredible," he exclaimed. "We've been playing this for two days, and it's kept paying and paying."

She added, "We've paid for our whole trip, airfare and everything. It's all been on the same machine."

Now, I've had players try to warn me off cold machines before, but I've rarely had players try to steer me to hot ones. For one thing, slot machines don't stay hot that long, and, for another, players who are winning want to keep the machine for themselves. I figured these players were probably shills on the casino payroll, playing a souped-up machine and letting other customers know they were winning in hopes of drawing them into spending their money on the regular slots.

I decided to take a walk back a few hours later and see if they were still there. If they were shills and they were gone, the machine probably would be shut down. No way would the casino let regular Joes play a machine that had been fixed so house players would appear to be winning.

They were gone, but the machine was still open. With that, I figured they were legitimate customers on a lucky streak. It probably wouldn't give me those results, but it was just possible that they'd accidentally hit upon a real rarity—a machine with a payback percentage that made really long winning streaks possible.

I took out a $20 bill and started to play. And the 10 minutes I took to lose it was all the trial I gave it.

The bottom line is that tips from other customers about hot and cold machines, or any results you've observed yourself, have no bearing on how the slots will perform for you.

18. C. As of late 2003, Nevada had been replaced as king of the slot payouts by Colorado's low-limit casinos. Nevada's dollar slots pay out about 95.5, roughly the same as Colorado. Mississippi also exceeds 95 percent, as do some Illinois and Iowa casinos. Colorado's low-limit slots actually exceed Nevada paybacks on quarters, averaging in excess of 94.5 percent while Nevada hovers around 94, with Missouri and Iowa paying out 93 percent or a little better. And on nickels Colorado is again top of the mountain, averaging close to 93 percent payback, with Nevada a little less than 92 and Iowa in excess of 91.

Now, some places in Nevada still have higher returns than Colorado or anywhere else, as we'll see in No. 19.

19. C. Casinos in north Las Vegas have the highest-paying slots—or at least they have the best-paying electronic gaming devices. Nickel games average 93 percent, compared with 90 percent on the Strip. Quarter machines average better than 96 percent paybacks, and dollar machines more than 97 percent. Compare that to 93 percent on quarters and less than 95 percent on dollars on the Strip. Even the downtown Las Vegas figures of 91 percent on nickels, close to 95 percent on quarters and a few tenths of a percent better than that on dollars don't measure up to north Las Vegas.

But there's a bit of a statistical illusion at work. Remember back in the opening chapter of this book, when we defined "slot machines" and "electronic gaming devices"? Slot machines are electronic gaming devices, but electronic gaming devices include more than slots—video poker, video blackjack, video keno and some oddball games also are included.

In most jurisdictions, slot machines make up 80 percent or more of electronic gaming devices. We can take payback percentages for the Las Vegas Strip, Mississippi and New Jersey and be fairly certain they're giving us an accurate estimate of how the slots compare.

North Las Vegas is a different animal. Casinos there include the Fiesta, Texas Station, Santa Fe—they are not tourist destinations. Their primary customers are Las Vegas locals. And the game of choice among Las Vegas locals is video poker. Half or more of the electronic gaming devices in these casinos are video poker machines. Not only are they video poker machines, but some are the highest-paying video poker machines around, machines that pay more than 100 percent with expert play. Most players aren't experts, and the casino still makes a profit, but the return on these machines is still much higher than on reel slots.

That skews the percentages. Does north Las Vegas offer the highest paybacks on reel slots and video reel games? Probably. Maybe. But there's no way to separate the reel slot data out from all that video poker and find out for sure.

20. D. Two identical-looking machines don't have to have similar play characteristics at all. The hit frequencies could be wildly different. So could the frequency of top jackpots or the payback percentages. There's no way to tell from the outside.

Reel Spin No. 8: Narrowing the Edge

Slot machines traditionally have been games of pure chance, with an advantage for the house built into the odds. Some modern games have given knowledgeable players a chance to gain a little edge. It's more work than fun, and if you're going to concentrate on getting an edge you'll do more looking than playing.

Even if you don't go on an extended search for an edge, awareness of the answers that follow can help you stretch your budget:

1. **On the average, the house edge on slot machines is:**
   A. Higher than on table games.
   B. Lower than on table games.
   C. About the same as on table games.

2. **Compared with a table game with a similar house edge, slot machines produce:**
   A. More casino revenue per hour.
   B. Less casino revenue per hour.
   C. About the same casino revenue per hour.

3. **Sound money management at the slots:**
   A. Can help the player overcome the house edge.
   B. Can help the player narrow, but not overcome, the house edge.
   C. Can help the player limit his losses.
   D. All of the above.
   E. None of the above.

4. It's possible for a player to gain an edge on:
   A. Bonus slots.
   B. Tournaments.
   C. Both of the above.
   D. None of the above.

5. A player who has an edge on a slot machine:
   A. Will win frequent big jackpots.
   B. Will win every time he plays.
   C. Will make a profit in the long run provided he plays only when he has an edge.

6. When the player finds a machine that gives him an edge:
   A. He plays for a short time, then moves on.
   B. He plays as long as he can last between meals and naps.
   C. He moves into the casino hotel and supports himself on slot winnings and casino comps.

7. Bonus games can be profitable for the player if:
   A. The bonus is "banked."
   B. The bonus is launched by a single symbol landing on the payline.
   C. The bonus requires player skill.

8. A list of beatable bonus games includes:
   A. Piggy Bankin'.
   B. Fort Knox.
   C. Racing 7s.
   D. All of the above.
   E. None of the above.

9. A manufacturer whose games often offer lower house edges to players who have skill or knowledge is:
   A. IGT, with *Laverne and Shirley, M*A*S*H* and *Wheel of Fortune.*
   B. Mikohn, with *Ripley's Believe It or Not,* Clue and Battleship.

C. A.C. Coin, with Slotto, Hot Dog Express and Popcorn.

D. WMS, with Monopoly, *Survivor* and *Hollywood Squares.*

10. A reel-spinning game that adds an element of skill is:

A. *Wheel of Fortune.*

B. *Jeopardy.*

C. *Family Feud.*

D. Yahtzee.

11. A video game that includes an element of skill is:

A. *The Price Is Right.*

B. Battleship.

C. *Press Your Luck.*

D. Monopoly.

12. The greatest skill needed in slot tournaments is:

A. The knowledge to choose the right machine.

B. The ability to play fast.

C. A sense of rhythm.

D. There is no skill in slot tournaments.

13. A "100-percent equity" tournament is one in which:

A. All entry fees are returned to players in the form of prizes.

B. The field is 100 percent full, with entry fees enabling the casino to meet its advertised prize levels.

C. Players are given a certain number of credits to play with no time limit, so that all players have an equal number of spins and an equitable chance at the prizes.

14. It's better for the players if:

A. No money changes hands during play; the players accumulate points toward the prize money but don't get to keep anything won during the tournament.

B. The tournament is played with live money, and the players keep all winnings.

C. It makes no difference.

15. The player has the edge if a tournament:
    A. Offers 100 percent equity, regardless of format.

    B. Offers 100 percent equity and the entry fee includes all play.

    C. It is free of charge.

Reel Spin No. 8: Narrowing the Edge Answers

1. A. On the average, the house edge is higher on slot machines than on table games. A craps player faces a house edge of 1.41 percent on the Pass Line. That means, for every $100 a player bets, in the long run he or she can expect to lose $1.41. Per $100 wagered, an average blackjack player can expect to lose about $2, and one who learns basic strategy can narrow that expected loss to 50 cents. A baccarat player can expect to lose $1.17 per $100 if he bets on Banker and $1.36 per $100 if he bets on Player.

In exchange for a chance at bigger jackpots, slot players face a much bigger house edge. When we say that on the average, in downtown Las Vegas, quarter slots return about 95 percent and dollar slots a little less than 96 percent, we're saying the house edge is about 5 percent on quarters and 4 percent on dollars. In the long run, the quarter slot player can expect to lose about $5 per $100 wagered and the dollar slot player can expect to lose about $4 per $100. Outside Nevada, the house edge on slots is even larger.

There are table games with house edges that approach those on slot machines. Roulette players on an American wheel with both a zero and a double-zero buck a house edge of 5.26 percent; they lose $5.26 per $100 wagered. Caribbean Stud players, even those who know basic strategy, lose about $5.22 per $100 in antes in the long run. Some bets on the craps table are much worse—bet the proposition on Any 7, and you can expect to lose $16.67 per $100.

But, overall, the house edge at the tables is narrower than that at the slots.

2. A. Compared with a table game with a similar house edge, slot machines produce more revenue for the casino per hour. That's because we play slot machines much faster than we play table games. A roulette player at a busy table might see only 30 to 40 spins of the wheel per hour. Slot players who feed currency into the bill acceptors, play off credits and hit the "Max Bet" button to start the reels spinning again as soon as they stop can play as many as 1,000 spins per hour. I know—I've done it in tournaments.

I usually use 400 or 500 spins per hour as an average for a steady player. That's not breakneck speed, and it allows some leeway for players who take a walk to change machines or take a moment to chat with their companions or even take the odd bathroom break. Even so, that's more than 10 times as fast as roulette—if you bet $5 at a time for 40 spins of the roulette wheel and I bet 75 cents for each of 400 spins on a slot machine, you risk $200 and I risk $300.

The difference in speed means more money wagered and more revenue for the casino, even at games with similar house edges.

3. C. Sound money management can help a player limit his losses, but it can't overcome or even narrow the casino's built-in mathematical advantage on the slot machine.

I like to keep money management to a few simple principles:
Play only with money you can afford to lose.

Sure, you're going to win sometimes, and occasionally even have some big wins. But the most likely result each time we play is a losing session. That's what the house advantage and the programmed payback percentages we've been discussing are all about. When the inevitable losses come, you don't want the rent, mortgage or food budgets going down the slot. Treat a day, or a few days, at the casino as an entertainment expense. Then it's a thrill when the jackpots come and doesn't really hurt you when you lose.

Part of playing only with money you can afford to lose is never playing with borrowed money. The last thing you want is to be stuck with a big credit card bill, at credit card interest rates, for the sake of a little time at the slots.

Play within your budget.

If you walk into a casino with $100, you don't belong on dollar slot machines. Losing streaks are part of almost every session on the slots, and you don't want one bad streak to eat up your entire bankroll. You have to be able to weather the cold streaks if you want to be in action when things warm up.

How long you intend to play is a factor. Is your visit limited to a couple of hours? Then, with a $100 bankroll, you might start off on quarter machines. Do you expect to make it last all day? Better head for the nickels, and be prepared to take frequent breaks.

Take breaks.

Get up and stretch your legs. Watch the roulette wheel or the craps table for a few minutes. Go outside and get some fresh air. By all means, break for meals or even the odd snack. If it's not meal time, check out the menus and whet your appetite for later. Don't be a slot zombie. If you stare at the reels or video screen and push the button continuously, the house advantage works against you continuously. Better to take regular breaks, refresh yourself, clear your head and then get back to chasing jackpots.

Divide your bankroll into smaller session bankrolls.

If you're spending three days in Las Vegas and have brought $1,200 to gamble, divide your money into three $400 segments. On day 1, you have the first $400 to play with. If you win, great. If you lose it all, don't dip into the second $400. Quit for the day. Go listen to the band in the casino lounge, or take a walk up the Strip and watch the volcano at the Mirage and the pirate battle at Treasure Island. Do some serious window shopping. But you've already had your run at the slots for the day; make sure you have enough money to keep yourself busy tomorrow, too.

If you have money left at the end of the day, that's terrific. What to do with it is up to you. Many others advise putting that money away to take home, or to buy yourself a nice gift. I have no quarrel with that. I think every dollar of your gambling budget that you bring home is a nice morale boost. But if you want to add it to your gambling bankroll for the remaining days instead, that's up to you.

If you have $200 left of your $400 for day 1 and want to increase day 2 and day 3 to $500 each, hey, it's your money.

I do strongly advise that, when you have a moderate-to-big hit, you put at least part of that away. Hit a $1,000 jackpot, and make sure you take at least half of that home. Put it in your room safe, or with checked valuables at the front desk, and don't even look at it again until it's time to go home. Special treats at home are even more special when they're bought with money you won at the casino.

Don't play when tired.

I once chatted with the security director of Harrah's in Las Vegas, and he said they had a special category for people suffering from "Las Vegas disease." A player would faint or feel woozy and be brought to the infirmary. The first questions asked would be, "When did you last sleep? When did you last eat? How much have you had to drink?"

I know as well as anyone the adrenaline rush that comes from being in the casino, and many players think they can go on pushing the buttons and pulling the handles forever. But we're still human, and we have to take care of basic needs. If we play when we're too tired or too hungry or had too much to drink, our judgment is clouded. It's all too easy to give in temptation and play one more $100 bill than we'd intended when we're too tired to resist.

4. C. It's possible to gain an edge on some older bonus slots and in some tournaments. And there are slot pros with lots of time and very large bankrolls who play progressive machines for profit. But the average player should understand that the edge will be very small. You can hold your own on the slots, but don't quit your day job.

One of my readers once telephoned me about an interview with a slot pro they'd seen in *Midwest Gaming and Travel* magazine, for which I write a monthly question-and-answer column.

"Well, did you read about the slot pro? Making a living playing progressive slots? Is that possible?"

I did, and it is, although I suspect there was some oversimplification in the explanation.

"So tell me about it. Is this a way to beat the slots?"

It's possible, but it's not a way for just anyone to beat the slots. In fact, the article in question was careful to explain that this slot pro's system isn't for everyone.

"What's there that you or I couldn't do?"

First things first. Let's take a look at the system as explained by this anonymous pro. She says she charts jackpots on progressive games. She marks down the size of the jackpot every time certain progressive games hit the big one. After many readings, she gets an idea of the average size of the jackpot when it hits. She then plays the machines only when the jackpot hits that average size.

For example, if a jackpot starts building from a $1,000 base, but a chart of dozens, if not hundreds, of hits shows that the jackpot usually turns up between $2,500 and $2,800, she wouldn't start playing until the jackpot reached $2,500.

"And that gives her an edge on the game?"

That's not as certain as the pro makes it sound. It takes painstaking research. The machines have to be staked out and every jackpot charted until the sample is large enough to be a real indicator. That means being there every day for weeks.

At the same time, we have no way of knowing a machine's overall payback percentage. It's possible that a machine's overall payback percentage is so low that there is still a house edge on the game even when the jackpot is up in its average range.

If you take a progressive with a jackpot starting point of $1,000, and start playing only when the jackpot is at least $2,500, in the long run you will do better than those who play even when the jackpot is lower. But that doesn't necessarily mean you'll make money. It could just mean you'll lose less.

Beyond that, there is a big problem. It takes a *lot* of money to play this system seriously. There is no guarantee that a slot jackpot is going to hit in its average range. Slot results are as random as a human can program a computer to be. The odds of hitting on your next pull when the jackpot is $1,000 are the same as when the jackpot is $2,500 and the same as when it's $5,000.

We have no idea when the next jackpot is coming, and the player has no guarantee that he or she is going to be the one to hit it.

Also, progressive slots are notoriously low payers between big hits. So much of the overall payback percentage is tied up in the top jackpot that, for smaller hits, the machines must have either low pay tables or low hit frequencies, or both. That means the player loses money faster between big hits than on regular slots.

Taken all together, our slot pro isn't walking up to a $1 slot machine with a $100 bill and hoping to get lucky. For any serious jackpot-chasing, she has to be backed by thousands of dollars, and be prepared to lose it.

"The pro makes sure she hits the jackpot by using a team to monopolize a bank of slots."

Think how expensive that is. If a bank of 10 machines is tied to the same progressive jackpot, a team taking over the bank would need to be backed by tens of thousands of dollars, with tens of thousands more in reserve in case hitting the jackpot takes longer than usual.

"So you don't recommend charting and playing progressive slots?"

That depends. If you're already playing a game with a lower house edge—if you play basic strategy or better at blackjack, stick to the good bets at craps, bet Banker or Player at baccarat or play video poker well—you're giving yourself a better shot to win than you're likely to get on progressive slots.

If you already play progressive slots, that's another matter. You don't hurt yourself by waiting to play until the jackpot is large. You even help yourself a little, both increasing your long-term payback percentage a little and risking less by playing less.

But play progressives professionally, for profit? It's possible, for those with enormous amounts of time and money to invest, plenty of patience for charting jackpots and a willingness to lose tens of thousands of dollars waiting for the next big hit.

That's not for me, thanks, and it's probably not for you, either.

5. C. A player who has an edge on the slots can churn out a small profit provided he plays only when the odds are in his favor.

There is nothing a player can do to force big jackpots. If you're hunting for payoffs in the thousands of dollars—or even the hundreds of dollars—well, good luck to you. That's part of the attraction of playing slot machines. People like the idea that in the couple seconds it takes for the reels to spin, they could win enough to afford a life on easy street, or maybe to pay off the mortage or the car loan, or even just enough for a nice evening out.

It's a nice dream, and a perfectly good reason for playing the slots. There's nothing wrong with playing for entertainment, and the entertainment value of the slots includes the chance at a big jackpot. But this entertainment comes with an admission fee, and that fee is the fact that most slot players are going to lose most of the time.

A handful of players play for money instead of entertainment. It's not easy. It requires knowledge, discipline and a willingness to take a pass on even the most enticing, exciting game around if it doesn't show profit potential. And the rewards are small. We're looking for games that give us a chance to win a few dollars in a few minutes, not millions of dollars in a couple of seconds.

You may not want to make looking for an edge your exclusive method of play. Sometimes it's more fun to just take your chances and let Lady Luck do her thing. But, if you incorporate some of the information that follows into your casino routine, you'll find your overall results improving. You may even get to like looking for an edge as much as chasing jackpots.

6. A. When the player finds a machine that gives him the edge, he plays only as long as he has the edge, and them moves on. A machine that is potentially profitable for the player is not *always* profitable for the player. Learning to recognize the situations in which the machine does offer profit potential is the key to gaining an edge. This applies mainly to bonusing slots, where the player may have a small edge for a short time, as we'll see in the next couple of answers.

7. A. On some bonus games, any player can gain an edge if he knows what he's seeking. What he's seeking are bonuses that are banked—that is, the bonuses build in increments, and just how far the machine has gone toward the next bonus determines whether the situation is profitable.

Look for individual machines that players have left with those bonuses partly completed. With a head start to the bonus, you can get there without the investment it would take if you started from scratch.

Problem is, these machines aren't as common as they were in the early days of bonus slots. Bonus events have taken other directions, with random spins of wheels, turns of globes and choosing hidden bonuses on video screens having taken over the industry. These can be fun to play, but don't yield an edge for the player.

Still, there are games around in which players build toward a bonus. In WMS Gaming's Boom!, players accumulate firecrackers at the top of the screen, and, when they reach a critical mass, they start popping and the player collects a bonus. If you find a machine with firecrackers already accumulated up top, you have a head start.

Charles Lund's 1999 book *Robbing the One-Armed Bandits* is a terrific guide to just how it was done. Some of these machines are still in casinos, and you can check out bonus levels for a little advantage play, if not tremendous profits.

8. D. Piggy Bankin', Fort Knox and Racing 7s are early examples of beatable bonus slots. All were fairly widespread in the late 1990s, but are not common today.

I use those three as examples of different types of beatable games. Piggy Bankin' is a reel-spinning game with a banked bonus— the larger it got, the better for the player. Fort Knox has a video game-within-a-game, involving solving a coded sequence of numbers to open the vault for a bonus. Racing 7s put an LCD screen in the top box of a reel-spinning slot, with red, white and blue 7s "racing" to the finish for a bonus.

Now, you're not going to make a living off these games today. There just aren't that many of them left. But, if we understand the concepts of what makes them beatable, we know what to look for when other beatable games appear.

Piggy Bankin' was the first slot machine to raise a fuss among blackjack and video poker experts, analysts who are used to games in which a skillful player can get an edge. Stanford Wong, a Stanford University math professor and blackjack expert reported in his newsletter *Current Blackjack News* in 1996 that Piggy Bankin' was beatable. Others soon followed.

On Piggy Bankin', every time the player has three blank spaces land on the pay line, a coin is added to a Dotmation piggy bank on a screen at the top of the machine. When the player hits the Break the Bank combination, the dotmation piggy breaks and the player gets the amount held as a bonus. The bank is then reset to 10 coins and starts building again.

The key is to check the amount in the bank before you start. Wong suggested the break-even point was as low as 15 coins in the bank in dollar machines. My trial and error in the Midwest led me to believe the magic number was closer to 30, although that may have been largely because the overall payback on Midwest machines is lower than those in Las Vegas.

I tried the theory at Hollywood Casino in Aurora, Illinois, which then had a fair number of Piggy Bankin' games. I decided to play only if the bank showed 30 or more coins. First, I found a quarter machine with 43 coins in the bank, then on another bank of machines, I found games with 51, 37 and 36 coins. I broke all four banks, and even though I was only playing quarter machines, I wound up with a profit of $33.50.

A big payday? No, but a lot of fun, and a lot of satisfaction in beating the casino at its own game.

Fort Knox was different, one of the first games released on Silicon Gaming's Odyssey machines. Today, not only is Fort Knox a relic of the past, but Odyssey machines themselves have become rare.

The Fort Knox bonus round involved cracking a 10-digit code to open the vault at Fort Knox. When you see an Odyssey machine, touch the Fort Knox logo to launch the game. Then check out two strings of numbers, one above the other. The full 10-digit string is the code to be solved. The shorter string with it shows the digits that have already been solved in previous play, followed by blank space for digits to come. When a player came across a machine in which five or more of the digits already were solved, the player had the edge.

While you're there, check out other games on the Odyssey machines. Take Buccaneer Gold. While playing, you collect pirate daggers, and five of them bring you a bonus. If, when you start, you see three or four daggers already sticking in the ship's rail, it's time to play.

When video games were starting to rise, mostly on the strength of WMS Gaming's fishing-themed Reel 'Em In and games from overseas manufacturers Aristocrat and Atronic, leading slotmaker IGT came out with a compromise system called the Vision Series. Vision Series games have a color LCD panel in the upper right-hand corner of the machine. There are several different bonus games on the LCD panels, often themed to go with the game on the reels.

Racing 7s was designed to play off Red White and Blue. Three 7s—one red, one white and one blue—are on a track. A 7 moves up a notch each time a 7 of the same color lands on the payline on the reels. In some versions, the player gets 100 credits if the red 7 wins the race, 25 credits if the white 7 wins and 10 if blue wins. On other machines, the race is worth only 20 credits on red, 10 on white and 5 on blue.

Blue will win most of the time. On the regular reels, blue 7s land on the payline more often than reds or whites, and that gives blue a nice head start in the race. Keeping that in mind, the profit potential is in finding a game with blue close to the finish line. That seems to happen more frequently with the lower pay table. In one day in Las Vegas in 1998, I found three Racing 7s machines with the blue just one notch from the finish line. Playing one coin at a time, I hit a blue 7 to win the race on the first pull twice; the other time it took three pulls. That was a five-coin investment that yielded 15 coins. That's hardly Megabucks territory, but it was enough to pay for a couple of buffets—a nice diversion with a little profit.

9. B. Mikohn games such as *Ripley's Believe It or Not,* Clue and Battleship offer lower house edges to players who have skill or knowledge.

Mikohn's video games often include bonus rounds that ask the player trivia questions. I'm a trivia buff, so *Ripley's Believe It or Not* is a favorite of mine. Line up three or more "Believe It or Not" symbols on a payline, and it triggers a trivia question with multiple-choice answers—touch the screen to choose an answer. Choose the right one and you get a bigger bonus, meaning a trivia maven will get the most out of this game. Some questions are more difficult than others, and the game will sometimes give hints. Be sure to touch the parrot who hosts the round and other symbols on the screen—Mikohn likes to hide little extras in its games.

Mikohn uses the trivia concept in several of its games. Trivial Pursuit, of course, is loaded with factual fun. One of the bonus rounds in Clue gives bigger rewards for correct trivia answers. Even *Garfield* in its pie-throwing bonus uses trivia. The player selects a target, then answers a trivia question. If the answer is correct, Garfield hits the victim in the face with the pie for a bigger bonus.

10. D. A reel-spinning game that adds an element of skill is Yahtzee. There are both reel-spinning and video versions of Yahtzee with a roll-the-dice bonus round. On the video version, the round is played out on the screen. Reel-spinning games come with oversized dice in the top box, along with a lighted display showing bonus pay-offs for Yahtzee rolls such as straights, three of a kind and four of a kind, with the big payoff being for a Yahtzee—five of a kind. First, all five dice roll. Then the player selects dice to hold and re-rolls the others, then does it once more—three rolls, just as in regular Yahtzee. Players who know which dice to hold and which to roll will get larger bonuses in the long run.

11. B. A video game that includes an element of skill is Battleship. Mikohn now has several games in the Battleship line, but the bonus round in the original plays as much like the classic board game it's based on as any themed slot game I've ever seen. The round launches when the player hits octopus symbols on the first three reels. The screen with the reels fades out, making way for a screen that displays a grid and eight missiles. Four ships are hidden on the grid, and the player receives a bonus for each ship hit. With each hit the ship is revealed, and with each miss the word "Miss" is displayed in the targeted square, enabling the player to narrow his targets. The more ships the player sinks, the bigger the bonus. If the player sinks all four ships, the game moves on to another bonus round.

That's a little different from the Battleship board game in that it takes only one hit to sink an entire ship, and the player gets only eight shots instead of simply trying to sink the fleet in fewer shots than an opponent. But player skill in narrowing the targets and zeroing in on the ships makes a difference.

12. B. All you need to do to be competitive in slot tournaments is to play fast.

Players in slot tournaments have a set amount of time in each round to accumulate as many credits, or points, as possible. You affect the outcome by hitting the button as quickly as possible, so that the instant the reels stop spinning, you start them up again. The idea is to get in the maximum number of spins possible to give yourself the chance to accumulate the maximum number of points.

To give you an idea of how that works, let's look at an inexpensive tournament I played in at the since-closed Sands in Las Vegas in 1993.

The Never-Ending Slot Tournament was a standard Sands promotion for years, drawing hundreds of players each day until shortly before the casino was closed and imploded to make way for the building of the Venetian. For a time, the daily first prize was an orgy to sate the appetite of the most fanatical player—the choice of a $500 guarantee or one pull on each of the casino's more than 500 slot machines. When I played, the top was a flat $1,000.

For $10, each player got the chance to tap away at the button that spins the reels for 10 minutes, and to watch the points add up.

The only skill involved is spinning those reels as often as possible in the alloted time. The top 12 in the daylong competition came back at 11 P.M. to play another 10 minutes, with prizes ranging down to three free tournament entries.

About eight minutes into my qualifying round, I had more than 6,000 points, and drew the attention of an attendant.

"Looks good," she said. "Let's see those blue 7s once more just to be safe."

Continually tapping the button as we spoke, I asked how much it had been taking to make the finals.

"Yesterday 7,100 made it," she said. "Let's see those sevens!"

Seconds later, my third set of blue 7s lined up for 1,000 points, followed immediately by three triple bars for 120 more. Finally, time expired with 7,614 points on the meter, making me the leader on the board.

"Finals are at 11," the attendant said. "Come back around 10 to check the board."

When I returned to the tournament area shortly 10 P.M., the leader board showed me in ninth place, good enough to qualify for the finals.

At 11, the 12 of us took our places, and the tournament assumed a game-show atmosphere as an emcee took up his microphone and urged a small crowd that had gathered around to count down to the beginning of the 10-minute finals.

Shortly into the session, my first set of blue 7s hit, and I relaxed, as grateful for the 20 seconds to rest my wrist while the machine added the total as I was for the 1,000 points. About midway through the round, I hit a second jackpot, and was running neck-and-neck with the elderly man seated next to me.

When the third set of 7s came up, I was ahead of my morning pace, and knew I had a shot at the big prize.

"Once more," I thought, "and I'll take my chances."

With less than 30 seconds left, the 7s came once more. Two pulls later, time expired and I had 8,664 points—1,700 more than the gentleman next door.

And a split second later, I knew I'd won the thousand. Three other players gathered around, offering congratulations. They'd heard my 7s mounting up. And my entry fee turned out to be the best 10 bucks I ever spent.

13. A. In a 100-percent equity tournament, all entry fees are returned to the players as prizes.

That's a pretty good deal. Usually the sponsoring casinos will throw in a perk or two—a tournament T-shirt or a free buffet. That means the casino is actually spending money on the tournament, hoping that entrants will play elsewhere in the casino when they're not playing their tournament rounds.

14. A. It's better for entrants to be playing for points, with no money changing hands during play. Their entire risk is the entry fee they pay upfront; they can lose no money during tournament play.

In that format, the casino usually uses a tournament chip, which soups up the random number generator so that winning combinations turn up much more frequently than in normal play. Instead of three Double Jackpot symbols lining up on the payline once in a blue moon, you might see them three or four times in a 15-minute round.

When tournament play uses live money, the casino can't use a tournament chip. Entrants are playing machines that have a house edge, meaning that on the average they will lose money during tournament play. Not only that, but since the main skill involved in slot tournaments is to continually push the button to spin the reels as often as possible, players lose even more money faster than they would playing at a normal pace outside the tournament.

That kind of slot tournament isn't common—almost all casinos have long since come to the conclusion that it's a better promotion to use the tournament chip. Illinois is an exception. There, gaming board regulations require that all play in the casinos be for live money.

That has caused some consternation in Harrah's headquarters during its national Millionaire Maker slot tournaments. Harrah's sponsors regional competitions in all its properties across the country, then flies all the winners to one of its resorts and gives them complimentary meals and rooms while they compete for a $1 million prize and the title of World Champion of Slots.

The final, and almost all the qualifiers, use tournament chips. Except in Illinois.

I took part in the Millionaire Maker qualifier in Joliet, Illinois, in 1997. Harrah's did its level best to make it a fun experience for everyone, but it's just not the same when the jackpots are as rare as in regular play and entrants are losing money while they compete.

15. C, and maybe B. It depends on how you look at it.

If a tournament offers 100 percent equity and the entry fee includes all play, it is a standoff from a monetary standpoint. If you played only in such tournaments from now until the end of time, the most likely result is that you would break even.

You can consider yourself to have an edge on the tournament if you wish to include the value of free T-shirts, tournament gifts, buffets or whatever else the casino is giving away to go with the tournament.

If a tournament is conducted with live money, the player does not have an edge. Most players will lose money on their tournament play.

For a real edge—and a reel edge—look to the free tournaments. Not every casino offers them, but they're around if you're an active member of a slot club. (See Reel Spin No. 9: Slot Clubs.)

Within a few days of each other in 1998, I played first in a 100-percent equity tournament in which the entry fee included all play, then in a free tournament.

When I told friends, relatives and co-workers what I was about to do, they all had the same question: "A slot tournament? How do you have a tournament on slot machines? Is there any skill involved?"

There is little skill involved, other than a determination to hit the "Spin Reels" button as fast and as often as possible to yield the maximum number of spins in the time allowed. But, for my money, tournaments—especially in a cashless format—are the best way to play the slots.

The tournaments I played—one at Empress Casino (now the Horseshoe) on a boat in Hammond, Indiana, and the other at the Tropicana in Las Vegas—were cashless, meaning players didn't feed money into the machines. At Empress, players paid a $200 entry fee that included all play. All entry fees were returned as prize money to the top 10 and last place finishers. With more than 140 players, it added up to a grand prize of more than $14,000 for first place, with awards ranging down to $435 for 10th and $290 for last.

The Tropicana tournament was by invitation—having stayed there a few months earlier, I was invited based on my play. There was no entry fee, but the Trop kicked in more than $28,000 in prizes, ranging from $10,000 for first place to $25 for 250th. The last 10 finishers of the more than 800 entrants also received $25.

And, since they were cashless, both events used tournament chips and I got to see combinations I've rarely seen for live money. At Empress, I hit the three Double Diamonds in my first round; at the Trop, nearly everyone hit three Double Jackpot symbols at least once.

So how did tournament time, Indiana-style, compare with tournament play in Las Vegas? Let's compare:

Tournament extras: Empress treated players to a welcome brunch, and gave everyone a tournament T-shirt. Players could mix and match breakfast and lunch foods, with scrambled eggs, bacon and sausage in the same buffet line as salads, fruits, scalloped potatoes, baked chicken and ham.

The Tropicana gave invited players complimentary rooms for two nights. A welcome dinner buffet was set up poolside, with Chinese dishes served while a Hawaiian band played "Tiny Bubbles" and "The Huki-Lau Hula." At an awards brunch the morning after tournament play, chefs prepared omelets to order.

Tournament play: Empress used a bank of Double Diamonds machines, specially equipped with tournament chips. Players each played two eight-minute rounds, then the top 10 finishers were invited back for a third round.

Tropicana cordoned off more than 70 machines, all of different types when not in tournament use, and changed reels and glass to make them all Double Jackpot machines. Everyone played two 15-minute rounds.

Empress' equipment had a big edge on the Trop's. At Empress, when a player hit a winning combination, points were added nearly instantaneously and the player could go on hitting the button. The Trop's machines took time to total up the points. It took nearly three minutes to ring up the 2,500 points for three Double Jackpot symbols, meaning that any time a player hit the big combo, he or she sat idle for 20 percent of the round.

Ambience: There's no comparison between a big land-based casino and a casino boat, not even with a boat as big and beautiful as Empress Hammond. Space limitations were exaggerated when a storm the night before the Empress tournament damaged the lower-level boarding ramp. All boarding came through the same deck, forcing hundreds of customers down the aisle adjoining the tournament area. It was easier to move around with more to see and do between rounds at the Trop.

Bottom line: Both Empress and Tropicana tournaments ran as smoothly as can be expected when dealing with that many people. It was a splendid time in both events.

Reel Spin No. 9: Slot Clubs

Until the early 1980s, no one had even heard of a slot club. Now almost every casino has one. See if you know how slot clubs work and what they can do for you:

1. **A slot club is:**
    A. A group of slot players who organize group casino excursions.
    B. A casino system for rating players for comps.
    C. A security device placed out of an out-of-use slot machine to prevent unauthorized personnel from unlocking the front.

2. **The first slot club was founded:**
    A. At the Golden Nugget in Las Vegas.
    B. At the Golden Nugget in Atlantic City.
    C. At the Gold Strike in Jean, Nevada.

3. **Slot clubs usually track play using:**
    A. Cards with a magnetic strip on the back.
    B. A punch-in system for buy-ins at the change booth.
    C. Name tags so that a slot host can note how long a customer plays.

4. **Joining a slot club:**
    A. Takes an initiation fee and dues, usually about $10 the first year and $5 each year thereafter.
    B. Takes a one-time fee of about $20.
    C. Is free.

5. **Slot clubs usually award points that can be redeemed for comps on the basis of:**
    A. Time spent at the machine.
    B. The amount of money played.
    C. The amount won.

6. **Slot club points often can be redeemed for:**
    A. Cash.
    B. Complimentary meals.
    C. Complimentary rooms.
    D. All of the above.

7. **It is better for the player if points are awarded on the basis of:**
    A. Amount played.
    B. Amount won.
    C. It makes no difference.

8. **Slot club benefits:**
    A. Are pretty much standard from casino to casino.
    B. Are the same regardless of the type or denomination of machine played.
    C. Reflect the casino's marketing goals.
    D. All of the above.

9. **Some slot clubs reduce benefits if the customer plays:**
    A. Only reel slots.
    B. Video poker.
    C. Video keno.
    D. Video blackjack.

10. **Cash returns from slot clubs will give you an edge on the house:**
    A. Never.
    B. Frequently.
    C. Rarely.

11. Players can also get an edge if they consider the value of:
   A. Room and meal comps.
   B. Tournament invitations.
   C. Mail offers.
   D. All of the above.
   E. None of the above.

12. In addition to redeeming points for comps at the casino, slot club club members often:
   A. Get a higher payback on slot machines.
   B. Receive offers for further comps in the mail.
   C. Are given instruction by the casino on how to find the best-paying machines.

13. The casino will drop you from its mailing list:
   A. After six months without play.
   B. After one year without play.
   C. After two years without play.
   D. It depends on the casino.

14. The most common casino comp is:
   A. Free beverages.
   B. Free buffets.
   C. Free rooms.

15. Compared with a $5-a-hand table games player, the quarter slot player usually receives:
   A. About the same amount of comps.
   B. More in comps.
   C. Less in comps.

16. Points compiled in one casino can be redeemed at another casino owned by the same company:
   A. Always.
   B. Often.
   C. Sometimes.
   D. Never.

17. **A slot club awards the player one point for each $10 played. The player then may redeem 40 points for $1. The cash back rate is:**
    A. 2.5 percent.
    B. 1 percent.
    C. 0.25 percent.

18. **Slot players can maximize their slot club benefits if they watch for:**
    A. Double points days.
    B. New video games.
    C. Old mechanical machines.

19. **When the player's slot club card is in the machine, the machine's payback percentage:**
    A. Decreases to make up for the comps being awarded.
    B. Increases to reward loyal players.
    C. Stays the same.

20. **Players should use slot club cards:**
    A. Wherever they play the most.
    B. Wherever they are staying on a casino trip.
    C. Always.
    D. Never.

Reel Spin No. 9: Slot Clubs Answers

1. B. A slot club is a casino system for rating players for comps. They're also called player reward programs, and most allow players to be rated for comps at either slots or table games while using the same card.

For most of casino history, slot players were regarded as low rollers, too unimportant at the bottom line for the casino to give any extras or perks.

That made a dramatic turnaround in the era of computerized slots. With slot machines taking higher denomination coins and tokens and accepting multiple coins per pull that can be played much faster than an old mechanical slot, the casino has found that slot players are among their most important customers.

How important? A customer who plays dollar slots steadily is as important to the casino as a $25-per-hand blackjack player.

Let's take a casino that gives the player an average 95 percent return on dollar slots. Then let's bring in a strong slot customer, who bets the maximum on three-coin dollar machines. The player doesn't have to be a speed demon—400 pulls per hour will do nicely for our test. That's a pretty easy pace for someone who slides paper money into the bill validator and plays off credits.

At $3 per pull and 400 pulls per hour, the customer risks $1,200 per hour. That doesn't mean he's actually dumped $1,200 down the slot. Most of the $1,200 in wagers come through replaying winnings that are added to the credit meter. With a

95 percent return, the customer gets back $1,140, and the casino averages a $60-per-hour profit.

Now let's look at the $25 blackjack player. Mostly likely, he's sitting at a table with two or three other players, and playing about 100 hands per hour. (If we were using a $5 blackjack player, we'd have him sitting at a full table and playing 50 hands per hour; a $100 blackjack player we'd have sitting by himself and playing more than 200 hands per hour.)

At 100 hands per hour and $25 per hand, our blackjack player risks $2,500. If he's an average player, the house assumes it has an edge of about 2 to 2.5 percent. That puts the casino's expected average profit against this player somewhere between $50 per hour and $62.50 per hour.

Our dollar slot player fits right into that range. But, until fairly recently, the $25 blackjack player could expect free rooms, free meals and other perks. The slot player could expect zilch. A complimentary drink once in a while, maybe. But serious comps were for serious gamblers, and serious gamblers were at the table.

When it dawned on casino operators in the 1980s that slot players were having a big impact on their bottom line, they realized they had to find a way to reinforce customer loyalty. Comps were the traditional way to do that among table players, but table players were seated right where a floor supervisor or pit boss could keep an eye on their play and fill out a rating card. Slot players, on the other hand, spread out over a much wider area and moved frequently from machine to machine. A pit boss couldn't stand there and watch them play. So how could the casino know which slot players were in action enough to merit free meals or free rooms?

The answer was the slot club.

2. B. The first slot club was founded at the Golden Nugget in Atlantic City. In 1991, I did a survey of Las Vegas slot clubs for the *Chicago Sun-Times* Travel section, and I phoned Andrew Pascal at the newly opened Mirage. Pascal, who is the nephew of Mirage

Resorts' founder Steve Wynn, traced the history of slot clubs. "We created the slot club in 1982 in Atlantic City (at the Golden Nugget, since sold to Bally's)," he remembered, "and it worked so well that we brought it to Las Vegas at the Nugget in 1984."

3. A. Slot clubs usually track players by using plastic cards with magnetic strips on the back. They look just like credit cards. Slot machines are equipped with magnetic readers; just slide your card into the reader, and the machine starts tracking your play.

Some slot clubs use cards with punch codes instead of magnetic strips. It makes no difference to the player. You still slide the card into a reader; the reader is just designed to recognize the pattern of punchouts instead of reading the magnetic strip.

In the early days of slot clubs, some casinos used cards with no data encrypted, and there was no reader on the machines. The player showed his card at the change booth when buying coins to use in the slots. The attendant made record of the exchange, and comps were issued based on the amount of total buy-ins.

Such a system was an invitation for abuse; there was little to stop a player from buying in, wandering off on the slot floor and returning to make another buy-in without actually playing. So the system was refined at some casinos so that not only was the buy-in recorded, but also the player had to show a slot floorperson that he was actually playing. In effect, the floorperson rated the player for comps just as table supervisors rated blackjack and craps players.

From a player's perspective, there was too much space and too few slot supervisors to make that system work equitably. My parents returned from a trip to Las Vegas in 1991, where they joined two slot clubs. One was at the just-opened Mirage, and it was a modern, high-tech slot club with readers on the machines. The other was across the street at the Holiday Casino, where you had to get play rated by a floorperson. They found they couldn't get a floorperson's attention, and wound up not bothering with the Holiday's club.   .

Since then, the Holiday Casino has become Harrah's, whose Total Rewards slot club not only uses magnetic readers, but also lets the player use his accumulated comps at any Harrah's casino in the United States.

4. C. Joining a slot club is free. The closest thing to a fee is that some have an activation requirement. You must accumulate a set number of points on the card before you become a full member and can redeem the points. If you come across a club with an activation point, it's up to you to decide whether you're going to play enough in that casino to activate the card. If the answer is no, you're better off leaving and playing somewhere that will start the rewards immediately.

I join the slot club at every casino in which I play. The first for me was the Island MVP Club—now called the Winners Club—at the Tropicana in Las Vegas in 1988. My wife and I weren't even staying there—we were staying at Bally's, but were doing a lot of exploring and casino-hopping. The Trop advertised a free gift for joining the club, and, since we were extreme low rollers, free seemed like the right price to us. The gift, as I recall, was a sun visor. We didn't play much—there were things to do, other places to see. But, to our surprise, a couple of months later we received a flyer in the mail offering a discounted room.

Time marches on. I'm still a member of the Trop's club, but I've added the Stardust, Las Vegas Hilton, Harrah's, Treasure Island, Caesars Palace, New York–New York, Four Queens, Fremont, Fiesta, Sunset Station, Palms, Hard Rock—name a Las Vegas casino, and chances are I have a card for it. Dozens of cards. And that doesn't even include my cards from various casinos in Illinois, Mississippi, Louisiana, Iowa, Wisconsin, New Jersey, New Mexico and Indiana.

I don't stay active in every one; I concentrate on the places I like to play and stay most. But nearly every one has responded with some kind of perk, from free or discounted rooms to cash vouchers to free meals to 2-for-1 buffets. One of the biggest surprises came from the Flamingo Hilton, where I signed up for a card but never used it. The Flamingo still sent me room discount offers for more than a year before I actually used the card in a slot machine.

5. B. Slot clubs usually award points on the amount of money played.

Here's an example: At one casino on my regular route, I get a point for every $4 I play. So if I'm playing a dollar machine with two coins at a time, I get a point every two pulls. When I accumulate a point, the slot club reader flashes a message telling me how many points I've earned at that machine. If I've played $148 through the machine, it'll say: "Congratulations John! You Have 37 Session Points!"

Other systems give the player a countdown. At another of my regular haunts, it takes $100 in play to earn a point. If I put my card in a quarter machine, the meter on the slot reader will say, "400." That means I have to play 400 quarters to earn my next point. If I play three coins, the meter will count down to 397, and so on until I earn a point. It then displays how many points I've earned that session and resets the countdown to 400 quarters to the next point.

On really sophisticated systems, the slot club computer retains the countdown so that the next time the customer plays, he doesn't start from scratch. If I have a 400-coin countdown, and reach only 200 before either other commitments or my bankroll decide to go, the best systems will start my countdown at 200 the next time I play. But, on many systems, my countdown is erased as soon as I pull my card from the reader. The next time I play, I would again start from 400. There's a third type of system in which the countdown is retained by the machine. If I count down from 400 to 200 and leave, the next player who uses a slot club card at that machine picks up the countdown at 200.

Some systems go a step further and display how many total points the player has in his account. That saves the player from having to go to a slot club booth and ask just what he has coming.

A few clubs are more secretive. They give you no countdown, and no information on how much play it takes to earn a point. When you go to the booth, they won't give you a point total, they'll just tell you what benefits you have coming.

Which is better for the player? Hey, the more information, the better. If we know just what we're getting, we can make educated choices about where to play.

What do those points mean? We'll get to that in the next answer.

6. D. Slot club points can be redeemed for cash, complimentary meals, complimentary rooms and more.

More players redeem their points for cash than anything else, so let's look at that first. And, for the sake of comparison, let's stay with the previous example. In the first casino, I get a point for every $4 I play. I can then redeem 100 points for $1 in cash. That means it takes $400 in play to earn $1 in cash. The casino kicks back cash worth 0.25 percent of my total play.

At the second casino, it takes $100 in play before I earn a point. When I accumulate 18 points, I can redeem them for $5 in cash. That casino is giving me 0.28 percent of my play in cash back.

Cash-back rates are all over the map, depending on the marketing goals of the casino. In late 2003, the highest rate I knew of was at Jumer's Casino Rock Island in Illinois, which kicks a full 1 percent of play back to the player. Others, like Harrah's Mardi Gras in Missouri, return as little as the 0.1 percent; still others, such as the Palms in Las Vegas, return no cash at all. The method by which it is paid differs, too. At many casinos, you can redeem points for cash on the same day you play. At others, notably Atlantic City casinos and others that market to frequent visitors a short distance away, cash back is given by direct-mail voucher, requiring a return visit to the casino. Check out the details when you join.

Can a slot club with a low cash-back rate or no cash return at all still be a good one? Yes indeed. It depends on other benefits and what you're looking for. Frequent meal comps or easy hotel discounts or freebies are all part of the equation. I had a long relationship with the Tropicana in Las Vegas even though they returned only about 0.1 percent of play in cash. Free rooms and meals were easy to come by, and, for me as an out-of-towner, that had a lot of value. Las Vegas locals who aren't looking for rooms still will find value in slot clubs at casinos such as the Palms, which gives no cash back. Fairly generous meal comps at good restaurants keep the regulars coming back.

Regardless of whether you redeem your points for cash or hold them for credit against your hotel room, gift shop merchandise or anything else your club offers, it can pay to ask a slot host for meal comps separately. A slot host can write you a meal comp without deducting points from your account. You can have your buffet and your cash back, too. The host can also turn you down, but then you're no worse off than before you asked.

Here's the drill. After you've played for an hour or so, ask to see a slot host. A passing change person can call one for you. Ask the host nicely if your play merits a meal comp. Don't demand a comp—rudeness makes the decision to deny you a comp easy. The host can check your account, see how much you've played, and make a decision. If you're turned down, ask how much longer you need to play for a comp. If it's going to take longer than you'd planned to play, cash in points or buy your own lunch. Don't play more than you'd intended for the sake of a comp. You don't want to lose an extra $100 at the machine for the sake of a free $5 buffet.

7. A. If the coins-per-point rates are similar, it's better for the player if points are based on amount of play. A few casinos do base their awards on the amount won; instead of accumulating points with the coins you put into a machine, you accumulate money on the points you take out.

When I did my survey of Las Vegas slot clubs in 1991, I spoke with Linda Lewis of the Barbary Coast about its coin-out slot club. "We're geared toward tourists," she said. "We like it, and our customers do too, if they hit a big jackpot."

It's great for big winners. An acquaintance of mine hit a royal flush on a $5 video poker machine at the Orleans, west of the Strip in Las Vegas, for a $20,000 jackpot. He got enough points on one hand to vault to the top of the club's rewards table.

But, overall, slots pay out less than they take in, and if you're losing in a coin-out club you're not being rewarded for your play. Let's say one club rewards you with one point for every dollar you put into a machine, and another gives you one point for every dollar you win. You run $100 through each. In the first club, you get 100 points. In the second club, you get points equal to the return. If the slot you're playing averages 95 percent payback, then on the average you'll receive 95 points for $100 in play.

In the first club, you've received 100 points. In the second, you've received 95. If the redemption rates are equal, you'll get more from the club that awards its points on the basis of money played.

Not only that, if you hit a cold streak, you're out of luck. In the first club, you run your $100 through and you get your 100 points, no matter what. In the second, if you get no payback, you get no points.

It all seems a little backward. Coin-out clubs reward big winners, who already feel good about the casino because they've won. They shunt aside those who lose and could use a little consolation. It's almost as if the casino is telling you, "You can't beat us? Who needs you?"

8. C. Slot club benefits reflect the casino's marketing goals. Does the casino rely on out-of-town guests and have a bunch of hotel rooms to fill? Then look for an emphasis on hotel discounts and free rooms. Does the casino attract mainly local players? Meal comps seem to be the ticket. If the slot club can keep the player in the house with a lunch or dinner on the house, then just maybe the customer will play an extra hour or two after eating. Does the casino have a large base of big bettors? Then the slot club will be geared to dollar-and-up players. The Mirage, for one, doesn't rate quarter slot play for comps. Does the casino need to grind out its profit by keeping lower rollers coming through the door? Then look for inexpensive buffets with lots of 2-for-1 offers to quarter players and even nickel players.

For your best shot at extra perks, choose a casino that's looking to lure your type of play.

9. B. Some slot clubs reduce your benefits if you play video poker. Why? Because on the average, video poker machines have a higher payback percentage than slot machines. Some casinos don't want to give the video poker player both a higher return and the same benefits that go to those who play games with a bigger house edge.

Casinos also sometimes vary their slot club benefits on the basis of denomination played. To encourage play in higher-denomination machines, they'll give a better cash-back rate on dollar and above machines than on quarter machines.

Check it out before you play. If you're a dollar slot player, you're golden. *Every* casino needs your kind of play. But, if you play quarters or video poker, a little shopping around can increase your return.

10. C. Rarely will slot club cash back give you an edge on the house.

Slot club cash back really works best for video poker players, who have a variety of machines to choose from that return close to 100 percent with expert play. Take Jacks or Better video poker with a "9-6" pay table. (Video poker players will know that means a full house pays 9-for-1 and a flush pays 6-for-1). With expert play, the machine returns 99.5 percent to the player. If the slot club redeems points to return to players 0.5 percent or more of their play in cash, the machine becomes a 100 percent-plus game.

There are many video poker machines that pay just below or just above 100 percent to experts. (Those wishing a more complete discussion of video poker might like my *Video Poker Answer Book.*) Slot players don't have as many options, but slot club cash back can help narrow the edge even further than the bonus-hunting described in the previous chapter.

11. D. Even if the player loses money on a casino trip—and there will be more losing trips than winners—room comps, free meals, tournament invitations and more can ease the pain.

In the last chapter, I described a free tournament I played in Las Vegas at the Tropicana. I didn't win any money in that one, but my room was free for two nights, and there was a free welcome dinner buffet with entertaiment and a free going-away brunch for both my wife and me. What's the value of that? A couple hundred dollars? What's the value of the free shot at winning some prize money, even if I didn't win anything that trip? Take it all into consideration, and it's an inexpensive, fun vacation, even if things don't go well in the casino.

The key, of course, is to keep your head when you play. Don't bet extra for the sake of comps—that can quickly cost you more than the value of the comps. Stay within your budget, and play what you'd planned to play for your day's entertainment. Then take whatever perks come with it.

12. B. In addition to whatever their points bring them, slot club members frequently get offers in the mail for more good stuff.

Just what you get depends on the casino. Las Vegas depends on vacationers who spend a few nights. So room discounts and free rooms are frequent enticements.

It doesn't always take much play to start the offers coming. When I signed up for an Emperors Club card at Caesars Palace in Las Vegas, I made only about $100 in one machine. I took advantage of an offer for a free $20 if I played $50 with a new slot club card. I gave them a little more play than that. I ran $100 through a machine once, won $25 and picked up my free $20 for a $45 profit. No matter. I made the mailing list for room discounts.

But room freebies and discounts aren't all the casinos are offering; free meals, tournament invitations, parties, gift shop specials, prize drawings and more are among incentives casinos send by mail to try to lure you back.

In Atlantic City, where the majority of play is drive-in trade from New York and Philadelphia, casinos entice players with cash vouchers above and beyond anything they get from their slot club points. In the late '90s, I spent one night at Harrah's in Atlantic City. I had a good run on dollar machines, so I was able to play a long time in that one night. Apparently Harrah's liked my level of play. It sent an offer of an extra $250 in cash back on my slot club card.

Near my home base in Chicago, riverboat casinos and casino barges in Illinois and Indiana also rely on drive-in trade. At one point in 2003, I had on hand cash vouchers from Hollywood in Aurora, and Harrah's and Empress in Joliet on the Illinois side; and from Trump and Majestic Star in Gary, Horseshoe in Hammond and Harrah's in East Chicago across the Indiana border. Some also sent meal vouchers and offers of free hotel stays.

Is there anything to stop me from driving around, collecting the cash and not putting any of it back in the slots? Nope. My vouchers would just be skimpier in coming months.

13. D. How long it takes a slot club to drop you from the mailing list depends on the casino. As you go longer without returning, the generosity and frequency of the casino offers taper off. But I have gone three years or more without playing in a given casino, and been surprised when a room discount showed up in my mailbox. If your previous slot club activity shows them you like to play, they'd like a way to get you back.

14. A. The most frequent casino comp is free beverages. If you're playing, the cocktail waitress will ask if you want anything to drink. I've been comped cocktails in Las Vegas while playing nickels. Some newer gaming states have regulations against the casino comping alcoholic beverages. The states' powers that be don't want their citizens to lose their heads while playing, and, even more important, they don't want them driving home under the influence. If the casino doesn't comp cocktails, it'll probably still give you juice, soft drinks and coffee.

15. B. Quarter slot players usually receive more in comps than $5 table players. I once received a letter from a reader complaining that he played $5 blackjack, while his wife played quarter slots. She received cash back, complimentary meals and invitations to special events, while he couldn't even score a buffet comp.

He didn't realize that slot play is the casino's bread and butter.

Let's say that you're playing blackjack at $5 a hand. Tables with $5 minimum bets often are crowded, so we'll assume you're at a full table playing about 50 hands per hour. That means you're risking about $250 per hour.

How much of that does the casino expect to keep? The house assumes that its edge over an average player is about 2 percent to 2.5 percent—although a player who learns basic strategy can narrow that to about half a percent in a multiple-deck game. That means the casino expects to keep an average of 2 percent to 2.5 percent of your $250 in wagers per hour, or about $5 to $6.25 per hour. Sometimes you'll lose far more, and sometimes you'll win, but that's the average the casino expects.

Now take a slot player betting three quarters at a time at a nice, easy pace of 400 pulls per hour. With three quarters at a time for 400 pulls, the quarter slot player is risking $300 per hour—$50 per hour more than the $5 blackjack player. Not only that, but the house also keeps a bigger percentage on the slots than on most table games. Let's call the average return on quarter slots about 92 percent; it's higher in Nevada and lower in New Jersey, but this will do for most of the country. The house keeps about 8 percent of all money played. That leaves our quarter slot player with average losses of about $24 per hour—nearly five times the expected losses of the $5 blackjack player.

Naturally, with the quarter slot player contributing about $24 per hour to casino coffers while the $5 blackjack player yields only $5 per hour, the slot player is going to get bigger and better comps.

16. C. Points compiled in one casino can sometimes be redeemed in another casino owned by the same company. Harrah's Total Rewards card links all its casinos in the United States; you can earn points in North Kansas City and redeem for meals in Lake Tahoe. In Las Vegas, the Boarding Pass card from Stations Casinos unifies rewards at Palace Station, Boulder Station, Sunset Station, Green Valley Ranch Station, Texas Station and Santa Fe Station.

That's the wave of the future. There's been a big shakeout in gaming in recent years, with chains buying up formerly independently owned casinos. Eventually, most of the chains will find slot clubs an opportunity to cross-market, as Harrah's has done.

17. C. If the casino gives you one point for each $10 in play and you can redeem 40 points for $1, the cash back rate is 0.25 percent.

You can apply this basic formula to any slot club that gives you details on how you earn points and at what rate they're redeemed. Multiply the amount of play required to earn a point by the number of points it takes to redeem for a dollar. In this case, $10 per point times 40 points per dollar returned gives you $400 in play per $1 in cash back. Then divide the dollar return by the number of required points: $1 divided by $400 is 0.0025. Multiply by 100 to convert to percent, and the cash return is 0.25 percent of your play.

18. A. Slot players can maximize benefits on double points days— or better yet, triple points days or even quadruple points days. Alternatively, some casinos run occasional double-cash-back days. It amounts to the same thing.

Sometimes a casino will set days of the week in which they'll award double points. Other times they'll mail you coupons redeemable for double points after you've completed play.

Watch your mail and watch for promotional signs in the casino. Las Vegas visitors should check out the freebie magazines available in hotel lobbies and car rental agencies. Advertisements may alert you to a bonus-point opportunity. Ask about double-points days at the slot club booths. Even if your normal play merits only $5 in cash back, isn't $10 a nicer figure?

19. C. When the player's slot club card is in the machine, the payback percentage remains unchanged. The random number generator that determines the reel combinations is on a separate chip and does not know that you're playing with a slot club card.

Some players seem to like to attribute any cold streak to playing with the card. They take the card out, they tell me, and the machine heats up. But it's all random chance and selective memory. They don't seem to remember the times they've hit the good stuff with the card in. Any cold streak sends the player's mind racing, looking for a reason. And the basic reason is this: slot machines have cold streaks, club card or no club card.

Look at it this way. The casino is going to great lengths to insure your loyalty by offering you cash, meals, rooms and more. Is it then going to chase away a valued customer by shorting the return on the slot?

20. C. Players should use slot club cards whenever and wherever they play. Even if you're not going to play enough to earn any return on this trip, you never know what kind of bonus is going to show up in your mailbox later.

Reel Spin No. 10: The Readers Write

I get many letters from readers asking all manner of questions about casinos and gambling. The biggest share, naturally enough, is about slot machines. See if you can answer the following questions I've received from readers:

1. Are the credit and pull handles on slot machines on the same cycle? It seems whenever I let credits build up and push "Max Bet" I have bad luck. Is this just a coincidence?

2. Sometimes, when a player hits a big slot machine jackpot, it's paid by an attendant instead of by the machine. What happens if the player thinks the machine has broken, since it's not spitting out any coins? What if the player walks away? Is the jackpot lost?

3. I need the definitive answer on when and what is reported to the IRS as it applies to gambling winnings. Somebody just came back from Vegas and said they won $1,600 on a slot machine and had to sign for it! Not that I'll ever have this problem, but it's something to ponder.

4. Should you put in only a few coins in one machine, then move to another machine? Do you put your whole budget in one machine? Just how should one play it? Also, how are the machines programmed? Are they set to pay off once every 24 hours, for example? Is it a random hit-and-miss situation, where if in the right place at the right time you get lucky?

5. I heard of an incident in Mississippi where a woman hit for $11,000 on a dollar slot machine. Before they paid her, they asked if she had any magnets on her, did she have any lucky trinkets with magnets; they searched her purse and they frisked her. Also they told her it would be best that she left and they escorted her to the city limits. I would like to know why she received this type of treatment.

6. I've heard that in Las Vegas certain slot machines are souped up with a shill playing it. I thought that by state laws all slots are set paying out the same. Explain please.

P.S.: Can you play a souped-up machine after the shill leaves?

7. I recently won a large hand-paid jackpot at the slot machine. After I won, three men came, opened the machine and took a large board out of the machine that looked like it contained microchips. They used an instrument to use and test different parts of that microchip board.

Is that legal? I was always under the impression that the machines are programmed by the manufacturers and that no one could tamper with them.

8. I have gambled on slot machines approximately a dozen times. It appears that once a slot machine gives you a mid-range payout— $160 to $400—that's it. The machine goes cold. Have you noticed this or is it my imagination?

9. Are slot machine payoffs linked together? When a casino boasts of a 98 percent payout, does each individual machine know how much every other machine is paying out?

10. What does it mean when a casino advertises it has slot machines with up to 99 percent payback? I always seem to leave with a lot less than 99 percent of my money.

11. I have read where payouts on slots are random and also that slots are programmed. I suppose they are programmed to be random, which I understand.

I have also read that jackpots are programmed to pay out once per so many pulls. That doesn't sound random at all. What am I missing?

12. I recently observed an intriguing operation of several Triple Diamond slots by two technicians. They opened two of the machines, pressed a certain switch, ran credits on the meter, then proceeded to press the "spin" button. To my surprise, *every spin* was a jackpot, beginning with the highest and continued to the lowest multiple payout. What effect would this have on subsequent play?

13. I love the new five-reel slot games on video screens. It seems to me, though, that I get the second-screen bonuses more often when I play fewer coins. Also, are the second screens fixed so that you get low bonuses no matter what option you pick? I never seem to hit the big ones.

14. Why don't you tell the public what the real slot payouts are? Money in, money out at the handle, per individual player. I say the percentages are more like 6 percent and *not* 94 percent. How many pay 8 percent?

I do not argue the fact that in theory a slot set for an 80 percent payback will pay back 80 percent or a slot set for 97 percent payback will pay back 97 percent.

But I say money in–money out at the handle *per individual* is only 6 to 8 percent. How many *individuals* will run a slot machine through a full cycle? Theoretically, if a slot is set for an 80 percent payback over 100,000 pulls and takes $1 per play, an *individual* would have to put in $100,000 and pull the handle 100,000 times for a payback of 80 percent, or $80,000, which would be a loss of 20 percent, or $20,000.

No *individual* is going to put in $100,000 or pull the handle 100,000 times.

The average payback per *individual,* money in–money out at the handle is only 6 to 8 percent.

15. There are several things I want to know about the slots.

First, does the casino have control over the slot machine for it to pay off? I notice when my player's card is in I don't hit jackpots as much, but when I take the card out I do.

Second, I heard it took three hours to pay off a $25,000 jackpot because they had to check the machine all out before they paid. Could that be true?

Third, how are jackpots paid out? Do you have to pull so many times? Do you have to put in so much money to warm the machine up before it starts paying out?

Fourth, how can you tell when a machine is ready to hit? Does the machine have to make a certain sound, click or jerk before it pays out? Does a certain symbol (a cherry, 7s, etc.) have to appear in a certain position, which will let you know that a jackpot is about to pay out?

Fifth, do you have to have a lot of points to win?

Sixth, do player's card points accumulate from day 1 or just for that session?

Reel Spin No. 10: The Readers Write Answers

1. Yes, it's a coincidence if you seem to be getting better results by pulling the handle instead of pushing the button. I know the feeling—sometimes when I'm in a cold streak I switch to pulling the handle myself. But there is just one random number generator governing the reel combinations, and it makes no difference whether you hit the button or pull the handle.

2. If the player somehow mistakes for a malfunction all the flashing lights, screaming sirens and whatever other bells and whistles the manufacturer has programmed to celebrate a big jackpot, all may be lost. A player who walks away before being paid often forfeits the jackpot, which then reverts to the casino coffers.

All may not be lost if the player is using a slot club card. I was once talking with Don Wren, who then was the slot performance manager at Harrah's in Joliet, Illinois, and who later moved on to Harrah's in Las Vegas. He said Harrah's had managed to track down a player at home and pay a jackpot that would have been lost had the player not used a slot club card.

This will never happen to most of us—we won't mistake the signs of a jackpot, including the combination on the reels, for a sign the machine has broken down. But that player's experience, added to all the other benefits detailed in Reel Spin No. 9: Slot Clubs, is one more reason that a slot player's first move when sitting down to play should be to slide the club card into the machine's reader.

3. Casinos are required to report to the IRS any slot machine hit of $1,200 or more or any keno winnings of $1,500 or more. In addition, tournaments are held to be contests, and winnings of $600 or more must be reported by the casino. I ran into this last rule in Las Vegas when I won $1,000 in a slot tournament. Along with my winnings, paid in cash, I was given a form to fill out for the IRS.

Check out the payouts for top jackpots on slot machines, especially at the quarter level. You'll find a few that pay out $1,199—just $1 below the total at which the casino would be compelled to take identification of the customer and report the winnings to the IRS.

If you play in casinos with any frequency, it is a good idea to keep careful records of places and times you've played, amounts of buy-ins and amounts of cash-ins. All gambling winnings are taxable, but losses are deductible up to the amount of winnings provided you itemize deductions. If you use a slot club card, most casinos can verify the dates you've played. It is becoming increasingly common for slot clubs on request to provide printouts of your wins and losses for the year, although the IRS sometimes will not accept that alone as evidence of gambling losses. It's best to keep a detailed diary yourself, and use the slot club records as backup.

4. You have it right at the end—slot machines are a random hit-and-miss situation in which you win if you're in the right place at the right time. They are not set to pay off in anything as simple as a 24-hour cycle. If the random number generator is programmed to spit out a jackpot combination about once per 10,000 plays, in the long run that's just what it will do. But, in the short term, it could go 10,000, 20,000, even 30,000 spins without paying the jackpot, it could hit two or three times within 10,000 pulls or it could even hit twice in a row.

So in the long run it makes little difference if you stay at the same machine or move around. Personally, I prefer to move around if I have a little losing streak, but stay put if the machine's giving something back. But that's just for my own mental state—there's no way of knowing when a machine is going to hit.

Fairly lengthy losing streaks are common on slot machines, especially on older two- and three-coin reel-spinners. If I went 15 pulls in a row without getting any return on Red White and Blue or Double Diamonds, I wouldn't panic. That's the way the games are designed. Even a 20-coin or 30-coin hit for three single bars makes up for a lot of losing spins. If I'm playing a video slot that takes up to 25, 45 or more coins at a time, I'd be frustrated if I went more than five or six plays without getting something back—the bets are too large for a player's bankroll to sustain the long losing streaks they can manage on a two- or three-coin game. Those machines usually have high hit frequencies, although many of the hits bring a return of less than your investment. Still, even if you've bet 45 coins, get an 18-coin hit and lose money for the spin, you feel like you're getting something back to keep you in action.

5. In addition to the question asked here, the letter-writer included the name of the casino that supposedly frisked a woman, found a magnet and denied her a jackpot. So I called the casino, and I called the Mississippi Gaming Commission. Neither could find any record of any such incident. A representative of the casino said that an $11,000 jackpot would be large enough to be memorable at that property, and that one way or another the casino would have reaped a publicity bonanza. Either there would have been a publicity rush to the big winner, or the casino would have trumpeted the news that it caught a slot cheat.

On older machines, cheats sometimes used magnets to disable the timing mechanism and let the reels float until they could line up a winning combination. But today's slot machines are not so vulnerable to magnets. Casinos do not routinely check for magnets when a big jackpot is hit, but they may check the combination showing on the reels against the computer record of the pull. If they do not match, an investigation follows.

6. Before we get into the question of shills, let's be clear on one point: Machines are not required to pay out the same percentage, not in Nevada or any other state. Most states have a legal minimum payout, and some also have a legal maximum, but machines with widely different paybacks can be placed side-by-side in the same casino.

Now then, slot shills are not common, but you'll see them from time to time at some of the smaller Nevada casinos. Shills play special machines that return in excess of 100 percent. The casino hopes that potential customers who see the shills winning will be lured to try their luck at regular machines. The casino doesn't lose any money on the deal—the shills don't collect the money that comes out of the machines.

I once saw a man playing two adjacent $1 machines, hitting winning combinations on every pull. There were no credit meters in those days—on every win, coins came clanking into the tray. If you couldn't see what was going on, you sure could hear it. As one machine was paying out, he played the other. He was surrounded by dozens of racks of $1 tokens. The machines were roped off, and security guards stood at either end of the rope. Were those machines opened to all comers when this player left? Of course not. When a shill leaves, either he's replaced by another house player, or the machine is shut down.

7. While actually removing the board from the machine is unusual, casino operators can and must verify the game memory before paying a large jackpot.

One thing slot players should understand is that what's on the reels does not determine the jackpot. The reels are just a representation of a number that has been selected by the random number generator program on one of the microchips. If there has been a malfunction and the reels show a jackpot combination that does not correspond to the combination selected by the random number generator, then regulations do not allow the casino to award the jackpot.

Jackpot verification normally does not require removing a board from the machine. Because in this case the board was removed, I'd assume that at least one of the men who came to verify your jackpot was an agent of the state gaming board. In most newer gaming states the microchip that determines the combinations you see on the reels must be sealed in evidence tape. For it to be removed, a gaming board agent must be present to witness the breaking of the evidence tape, removal of the chip and the sealing with new evidence tape.

Slot machines' microchips are programmed by the slot manufacturers, but casinos are allowed to change the chips with proper witnesses and documentation.

8. We've all experienced cold streaks after a big hit. But, if we're being honest about it, we've also experienced cold streaks right from the outset, cold streaks after lukewarm streaks, even cold streaks after cold streaks. The fact is, there are a lot of cold streaks on slot machines. For the odds to work out right on reel-spinning machines, there have to be many more zero-pay pulls than winners. Five-reel video games ease the cold streaks a bit with frequent "wins" that are smaller than the wagers, but, even on the video games, cold streaks are a normal part of play.

Make allowances for that; after a moderate-to-big hit, put some of the money away, not to be replayed in that machine or any other. If you want to see if your hot machine stays hot, that's fine, but set a limit on the amount you reinvest. If you'd rather cash out and not take a chance on the machine turning cold, that's okay too. Either way, make sure you walk out of the casino with some of your winnings.

9. Machines do not know what percentages other machines in the casino are paying. Each machine is programmed with its own payback percentage, and it does not affect other machines.

If you see a 98 percent payback sign, don't assume all machines in the casino pay 98 percent. Usually, if you look carefully, you'll see the sign says "Up to 98 percent payback." That could mean one machine pays 98 percent and the other 1,000 in the house all pay less.

For a time, the Stratosphere Tower in Las Vegas advertised that all its dollar slots returned 98 percent. Such guarantees for a whole casino's complement are rare.

10. This goes hand in hand with the previous answer. "Up to 99 percent" doesn't mean that every slot machine in the casino pays 99 percent. There may be a handful that pays 99 percent, with others that pay 95 percent, 90, 85 and even less.

Even if you manage to find a 99-percenter, it won't give back 99 percent every time. That 99 percent is a long-term average—the machine will return to players 99 percent of all money played over a period of hundreds of thousands of handle pulls. Play 100 coins through a slot machine, and it's perfectly normal for even a 99 percent machine to have an ice cold streak and return 50 coins or less. There have to be losers to balance out the winners.

Not only that, but slot machines also pay back more even when you're losing than most players think they do. Remember back in "Reel Spin No.1: Definitions," when we discussed payback percentage and the effect of replaying your winnings? Let's say you start with 100 coins and play two coins at a time for an hour—on a machine with a credit meter, about 500 pulls taking 1,000 coins.

You leave with nothing. What was your payback percentage?

I've found many readers consider this zero payback, but think about it. The machine has given you enough payback to play 500 pulls. You've played 1,000 coins, only 100 of which were yours at the start. The other 900 coins are your payback for the hour. Even though you have nothing left, you've actually received a 90 percent payback for your play.

Combine the effect on your bankroll of replaying your winnings with the fact that a 99 percent machine doesn't necessarily give back 99 percent in the short term, and you'll see that it's possible to have played a 99-percenter without even realizing it.

11. Slot jackpots are programmed to hit once per so many pulls only in the same sense that any other casino game is "programmed" to pay out once per so many hands. The jackpots occur randomly, but the odds of the game are set up so that, in the long run, they will hit an average of once per so many pulls.

Let's start by using blackjack as an example. Given the proportions of Aces and 10-value cards in a standard deck, two-card totals of 21—blackjacks—occur about once per 21 hands. Sometimes they occur more frequently—I've had as many as four in a row—and sometimes you can play all day without one. But the odds of the game are "programmed" so that a randomly shuffled deck in the long run will produce one blackjack per 21 hands.

It's similar with slot machines. The program may be set up so that you'll get the small payoff on three mixed bars an average of once per 20 pulls. But sometimes you'll get them twice in a row, and sometimes you'll go 40 plays without them. When all results for all players over a long time are added up, the machine will have paid three mixed bars about once per 20 pulls, just as programmed.

12. The technicians were running a test program. Slot machines are cleaned periodically, and in the process the reels can be moved slightly. The test is run to be certain the symbols still line up in their proper position on the pay line.

This has nothing to do with customers' results when the machine is running in the regular play mode. That fact that the highest jackpot combination showed on the reels during the test program's run does not affect the timing of when that jackpot might turn up for real. Your results would still be determined by the random number generator built into the slot machine's programming.

13. The number of coins played has nothing to do with how frequently you get the second screen on a video slot. Just as on any slot game, a random number generator program run by the machine's microprocessor determines reel combinations. That random number generator does not know how many coins you've played.

Results of your bonus round also are determined by the random number generator. You will receive low-end bonuses more frequently than bigger jackpots, just as you receive small paybacks on the reels more often than you hit big ones. On a regular three-reeler, you hit three bars a lot more often than three 7s, right? Same with bonus games. There are a lot more random numbers being generated that correspond to 20-coin payoffs than to 200-coin jackpots.

14. Think about what a 6 percent payback would mean. Let's say you play steadily for a two-hour session, which would give you about 1,000 pulls. At $1 per pull, you're investing $1,000. If you're getting back only 6 percent, your return is only $60, and you lose $940.

Have you ever lost $940 in two hours, playing $1 at a time? I haven't, and I'd like to see the machine that holds that much.

The average payback per individual at the slots is a lot closer to 94 percent than 6 percent—the average player can expect returns, not losses, of $940 per $1,000 played in many gaming states, and can expect even more in Nevada. How could it be otherwise when the overall payback is 94 percent? That overall total is just an aggregate of all the individuals. There's nothing "in theory" about it. Those are the actual returns, reported each month by various state gaming boards.

Within that 94 percent overall return, there's room for a lot of short-term variation. It's not outside the realm of probability that you could lose $500 instead of $60 in two hours. Sometimes you'll lose less than $60; sometimes you'll win money. It all balances out, so that in the long run you'll get back $940 per $1,000 invested.

The more you play, the closer your results will approach the overall average. Let's say your community group takes a couple of buses with 100 players to the casino. All 100 play $1 at a time in the slots for two hours. Now your group is taking 100,000 pulls and risking $100,000. Your group's return is likely to approach $94,000, meaning the group as a whole loses about $6,000, or $60 per person. Some individuals will lose more than that, some will win, and someone may even win thousands. But the overall return, and the average return per individual, will be about 94 percent.

An added note: When I received this letter, I asked the writer to give me the type, location and number of a specific non-progressive two-coin or three-coin machine, denominations of $1 or less, that he thought paid only 6 percent per individual. I volunteered to play it with my own money for 1,000 pulls, or until my return exceeded his 6 percent figure per 1,000 pulls. For example, if he sent me to a two-coin, $1 machine, in which 1,000 pulls at maximum coins bet would take $2,000, I would play until I got 6 percent of $2,000, or $120, in paybacks. Then, I said, I would report back on the results for this individual.

If he was right, I could expect to lose $470 on a two-quarter machine, $705 on a three-quarter machine, $1,880 on a two-coin $1 machine or $2,820 on a three-coin $1 machine. It would be an expensive lesson for me.

There was no expensive lesson. He never responded.

15. Let's take the answers to this reader's questions one at a time:

1. The casino cannot control when a jackpot hits, nor does using your slot club card make a difference in your result. The mechanism for tracking slot club points is separate from the random number generator that determines reel combinations. If you have been winning more without your card, it is entirely by coincidence.

2. It normally takes 15 minutes, perhaps half an hour on a busy weekend night, to pay off a large jackpot. The combination on the reels does have to be checked against the computer record of the pull, but that doesn't normally take anywhere close to three hours. Only if there is reason to suspect an irregularity would paying off a jackpot take so long.

3. Jackpots are hit entirely at random—or as close to random as a person can program the random number generator to be. You're as likely to hit on your first pull as on your 10,000th.

4. The machine gives no signal that it is ready to hit. You cannot tell by looking or listening to a machine whether a winning combination will come up.

5. You don't need any points to win. I know of one woman who hit for $5,000 on the first pull she ever took on a slot machine. Of course, I know of many more people who have played for years without ever winning more than a few hundred dollars.

6. Slot club points accumulate every time you play and are held in an account for you until you redeem them. The casino does not wipe the slate clean each time you leave. Some slot clubs do have expiration dates on your points. You are allowed a few months or a year or two to redeem them, and then they disappear. Others have no set expiration date, although the casinos reserve the right to change programs at any time.

Bibliography

When I search for the answers to my casino questions, I've found many publications invaluable. The following are books I highly recommend on slot machines, casino comps and slot clubs:

Slot Machines: A Pictorial History of the First 100 Years by Marshall Fey, Liberty Belle Books, 2925 West Moana Lane, Reno, NV, 89509. $29.95.

Break the One-Armed Bandits by Frank Scoblete, Bonus Books, 875 North Michigan Avenue, Suite 1416, Chicago, IL 60611. $11.95.

The Slot Expert's Guide to Playing Slots by John Robison, Huntington Press, 3687 South Procyon Avenue, Las Vegas, NV 89103. $16.95.

The Frugal Gambler ($12.95) and *More Frugal Gambling* ($14.95) by Jean Scott, Huntington Press, 3687 South Procyon Avenue, Las Vegas, NV 89103.

The Las Vegas Advisor Guide to Slot Clubs by Jeffrey Compton, Huntington Press, 3687 South Procyon Avenue, Las Vegas, NV 89103. $12.95.

Other Books by John Grochowski

The Casino Answer Book, Bonus Books, 875 North Michigan Avenue, Suite 1416, Chicago, IL 60611. $12.95. In the same question-and-answer format used in *The Slot Machine Answer Book,* John Grochowski takes readers through the ins and outs of blackjack, video poker and roulette.

The Video Poker Book, Bonus Books, 875 North Michigan Avenue, Suite 1416, Chicago, IL 60611. $14.95. What video poker games are best for the player? How do strategies change when pay tables change? John uses the question-and-answer format to walk the reader through types of games and strategy differences.

The Craps Answer Book, Bonus Books, 875 North Michigan Avenue, Suite 1416, Chicago, IL 60611. $13.95. No game offers the player more betting options than craps. John's questions and answers guide players through the good, bad and ugly sides of one of the most exciting of casino games.

Gaming: Cruising the Casinos with Syndicated Gambling Columnist John Grochowski, Running Count Press, P.O. Box 1488, Elmhurst IL 60126, or call Huntington Press at (800) 244-2224. $11.95. A compilation of 67 essays on casino gambling, from blackjack to baccarat and slot clubs to progressive betting.

Winning Tips for Casino Games, Publications International, 7373 N. Cicero Avenue, Lincolnwood, IL 60646. $4.99. This 144-page small-format paperback is a basic primer on how to play casino games.

The Experts' Guide to Casino Games, edited by Walter Thomason, Lyle Stuart Publishing, New York, NY 10022. $16.95. John is one of eight co-authors, and provides a brief history of gaming in the United States as well as a chapter on blackjack. Other co-authors are Frank Scoblete, Henry Tamburin, Walter Thomason, Alene Paone, Steve Bourie, Jim Hildebrand and John Rainey.

About the Author

John Grochowski has been dubbed "Mr. Midwest Gaming" by Walter Thomason, editor of *The Experts' Guide to Casino Games.* His columns on casino games appear weekly in the *Chicago Sun-Times* and also appear in other newspapers and on the Internet. He's the monthly Answer Man, tackling questions from readers, in *Midwest Gaming and Travel* magazine.

This revised edition of *The Slot Machine Answer Book* is one of four in his Answer Book series with Bonus Books, along with *The Casino Answer Book, The Video Poker Answer Book* and *The Craps Answer Book.* The fifth book in the series, *The Video Slot Machine Answer Book,* is soon to be published. John also is author of the self-published *Gaming: Cruising the Casinos With Syndicated Gambling Columnist John Grochowski,* which collects many of his columns, and the basic how-to-play guide *Winning Tips for Casino Games.*

A regular in *Slot Manager, International Gaming and Wagering Business* and *Midwest Gaming and Travel* magazines, John is a popular speaker at seminars. He lives in the Chicago area with his wife and son.

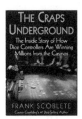